INTERNATIONAL COUNTERTRADE

Recent Titles from Quorum Books

INTERNATIONAL COUNTERTRADE

Edited by
CHRISTOPHER M. KORTH

QUORUM BOOKS
New York • Westport, Connecticut • London

Library of Congress Cataloging-in-Publication Data

International countertrade.

    Results of a conference held at the College of
Business, University of South Carolina, Spring,
1985; co-sponsored by the U.S. Dept. of Education.
    Includes bibliographies and index.
    1. Countertrade—Congresses. I. Korth,
Christopher M. II. University of South Carolina.
College of Business Administration.
III. United States. Dept. of Education.
HF1410.5.I5716 1987   382   86-25319
ISBN 0-89930-213-0 (lib. bdg. : alk. paper)

Library of Congress Catalog Card Number: 86-25319
ISBN: 0-89930-213-0

First published in 1987 by Quorum Books

Greenwood Press, Inc.
88 Post Road West, Westport, Connecticut 06881

Printed in the United States of America

The paper used in this book complies with the
Permanent Paper Standard issued by the National
Information Standards Organization (Z39.48-1984).

10 9 8 7 6 5 4 3 2 1

Contents

PART VII. OFFICIAL PERSPECTIVES TOWARD COUNTERTRADE

Exhibits

Preface

The exchange of one product for another is called "countertrade" (CT) or "barter." CT plays a major role in both domestic and international business. It has been estimated that more than 65 percent of the Fortune 500 companies have engaged in barter. Also, most governments of the world, including that of the United States, actively engage in countertrade; indeed, some governments *demand* that foreign companies accept local goods in exchange for their products.

Estimates of the portion of international trade that involves countertrade range from 5 to 20 percent—and higher. It is actually impossible to obtain an accurate estimate of the total volume of barter trade that occurs, either domestically or internationally. Such data is simply not gathered by any institution on any basis other than occasional, and incomplete, surveys. Nevertheless, it is widely recognized that the magnitude of countertrade is very large. In some industries and in some parts of international trade, it is quite prevalent.

Interest in countertrade has grown rapidly in recent years. Many seminars and a few books have appeared for the purpose of informing interested people, in both the private and government sectors, about the basics and some of the modern wrinkles of this old tool. The University of South Carolina presented a seminar that focused only on the international aspects of countertrade. The seminar was directed to those who were already familiar with the basics and who wanted more detail regarding current countertrade practices in various parts of the world and different industries plus insiders' views of many different aspects of the operations of a countertrading company and the attitudes of different official agencies.

The conference was held at the College of Business of the University of South

Carolina. It was cosponsored and partially financed by a grant from the U.S. Department of Education. I especially want to thank the U.S. Department of Education for its generous support and one of my colleagues, W. Randolph Folks, Jr., who was the manager of the contract under which the conference was held.

The chapters in this book are based upon the presentations that were given at that conference. The content has been edited for consistency between the writers and to orient the presentations for a reading audience. However, the presentations are essentially the same as presented at the conference.

The book is organized into seven sections:

I. INTRODUCTION: An overview of countertrade and of various countertrade practices in different regions and industries

II. COUNTERTRADE PRACTICES IN DIFFERENT REGIONS OF THE WORLD: A focus upon CT in Latin America, Western Europe, and China

III. COUNTERTRADE PRACTICES IN DIFFERENT INDUSTRIAL SECTORS: A focus upon CT in the project development, aerospace, and consumer-products industries

IV. RECENT DEVELOPMENTS IN THE TECHNICAL ASPECTS OF COUNTERTRADE: A study of financial, legal, operational, and strategic aspects of CT and a proposal for the development of a marketable security for CT credits

V. FACILITATORS OF COUNTERTRADE: An examination of CT traders, switch traders, and merchants

VI. TAX AND ACCOUNTING ASPECTS OF COUNTERTRADE: Views of an accountant, a tax lawyer, and the Internal Revenue Service

VII. OFFICIAL PERSPECTIVES TOWARD COUNTERTRADE: Views from the U.S. Congress and the U.S. Department of Commerce, as well as international views from the World Bank and the General Agreement on Tariffs and Trade (GATT).

PART I

INTRODUCTION

1

An Overview of Countertrade

CHRISTOPHER M. KORTH

This book covers a wide range of perspectives on countertrade: varieties; practices in different industries; practices in different parts of the world; various managerial considerations—finance, marketing, accounting, taxation, organization, and so on; and various specialized companies that can assist the company that wants or needs to countertrade. The authors represent both a cross-section of the entire industry worldwide and a variety of official agencies.

In this chapter a broad overview of the field of countertrade is given as a general background for those with a limited knowledge of the field.

DEFINITIONS

The first issue that needs to be addressed is that of semantics. Countertrade is a relatively new development for most of the companies and governments that are now involved in it. Although the basics are old—indeed, countertrade is the oldest method of business transaction—its modern sophistication is new, which is the principal interest of this book. Modern, commercial countertrade is also very international in scope.

As a result of these circumstances, the field of countertrade is weak in terms of its structure and systematic procedures. It is also weak with respect to terminology. As will be seen in the various chapters, there are sometimes ambiguities in terms of the exact meanings of the specialized vocabulary that is employed; this section discusses the various basic concepts. Also, when the terms are used in the following chapters, each author's specific meaning of the various terms will be made clear and his or her approach will be integrated, as much as possible, with the broad overview given here.

Countertrade

Countertrade is a relatively new term. Basically, it means the same thing as barter. *Barter* is the traditional term. However, some people think that barter has a primitive, even a negative, connotation. Some equate barter with the one-on-one exchanges in Indian markets in the middle of the jungle. Others see it in terms of efforts in the underground economy to evade taxes.

As a result of these image problems, many corporate financial and marketing or purchasing managers have encountered difficulty in convincing senior management to have an open mind about bartering. A new term can sometimes avoid the negative value judgments of older, more traditional terms. Therefore, the term *countertrade* is becoming more widely used. Both terms are widely used, however, and both are used in the following chapters.

Another reason for the use of a newer term is that there is little similarity between the primitive types of barter with which most people would be familiar and the sophisticated versions that are discussed in this book. Here, the authors discuss many modern refinements that require qualification to be understood clearly.

Simple Barter

Barter takes many forms. However, the essence of any type of barter transaction is simply the exchange of one product (whether a good or a service) for another (e.g., one antelope hide for so many ears of corn, or your help in building my fence in exchange for my help in painting your house, or a shipload of oil in exchange for fertilizer). This type of exchange is what is known as *simple barter* (or *straight barter* or *pure barter*) as opposed to some of the much more sophisticated modern variations that are described later.

Deferred payment: Traditionally, barter transactions occurred simultaneously (e.g., three of my sheep in exchange, at the same time, for one of your cows). However, even in primitive markets, deferred-payment arrangements could be made (e.g., one sheep a month in exchange for 100 bushels of wheat after the harvest). This type of agreement created a type of barter credit.

Multiproduct trade: The barter transaction could involve not simply the exchange of one good or service by each seller but several, or many, on either side (e.g., beaver skins and deer pelts in exchange for grain, coffee, blankets, and tobacco). Since many products are not readily divisible (e.g., a dairy cow) and the seller's demand for the other's principal product may be limited (e.g., eggs), the expansion of the trading to include a variety of products greatly increases the flexibility of barter. (When combined with the aforementioned barter credits, multiproduct trade becomes even more flexible.)

EXHIBIT 1.1

MULTILATERAL BARTER

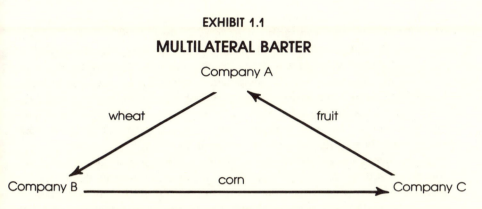

Multilateral barter: Another method in addition to multiproduct barter for circumventing some of the inherent limitations of barter caused by the restricted need each party commonly has for the other's goods or services is *multilateral barter*: several parties exchange goods. For example, Company A's wheat could be shipped to Company B, whose corn goes to Company C in exchange for fruit that is, in turn, shipped to Company A. (Exhibit 1.1.)

Thus barter can involve both goods and services. It may involve only two goods or services or many. It may involve two participants or several or many. It may involve simultaneous exchange or delayed compensation.

With simple barter, there is a direct exchange of goods between two parties. Only a single contract is signed. (In many of the informal deals, no contract at all is signed.) The agreement (whether written or oral) will specify both the specific type and the quantity of the goods or services to be traded. No middlemen are typically required. The goods or services will not be transferred to third parties. No money is involved (except indirectly, since in monetary economies both parties will tend to bear in mind some approximate monetary value for both products offered and products received). Such simple ''pure barter'' is relatively rare today.

Parallel Barter

A refinement over simple barter is *parallel barter*, or *counterpurchase barter*. It is essentially an adjustment to the fact that many companies will sell only in exchange for money (primarily hard currency); this could be for reasons of accounting practice, customs or exchange requirements, tax law, bank demands, or simply corporate policy. For example, commercial banks and government export-finance agencies commonly refuse to provide financing unless a contract provides for monetary compensation.

Under a parallel-barter agreement, two separate contracts, which specify the goods and services to be exchanged, will be signed. These goods or services are commonly, but not necessarily, of equal value. In addition, payment on each contract will need to be made with money (although frequently the means to pay on at least one side of the contract results from either barter-trade credit or bank credit.) Sometimes a parallel-barter agreement obligates one party to assist the other company in selling its products abroad.

Such arrangements are a form of barter because the two parallel contracts require a *quid pro quo* exchange of goods or services. Parallel barters are the predominant form of international countertrade today.

Offset: A special variety of parallel-barter arrangement is often called an "offset." For example, Northrop and General Electric committed themselves to market $150 million of Swiss goods as part of a $500 million contract for F–5 fighter aircraft. The offset could be either greater or smaller than the sale that was offset. Duke Golden discusses offset in detail in chapter 7.

Clearing-Account Barter

A more flexible format than either straight or parallel barter is clearing-account barter (or simply clearing arrangements). With clearing-account barter, each party agrees in the single contract to purchase a specified value of goods or services from the other country over a specified, often lengthy, period. Thus trade may be out of balance at the end of the first or even several years but will balance over the term of the contract.

Furthermore, this clearing-currency credit can often be used only within one country (although it can often be sold or transferred or switched to a third party). It is, in effect, a line of credit of a fixed amount, which is matched by a compensating line of credit in the other country. No money is actually involved in the trades in such barters. Each company or government thus provides the other with barter credits.

Frequently, clearing dollars can be used to purchase any of a variety of products. In other cases they can buy only a specified product. Nevertheless, clearing-account barter generally allows greater flexibility to either or both parties in terms of both time of drawdown on the "lines of credit" and types of products available. This form of barter occurs mostly between Communist countries or between a Communist and a less-developed country (LDC). It is, however, becoming more common between LDCs. However, there is nothing in the nature of clearing-account barter that would logically prevent it from being used by two private-sector companies in industrialized countries.

Buy-Back Barter

The fourth basic type of barter is a very special form that has evolved primarily in response to the reluctance of Communist countries to permit ownership of productive resources by the private sector—especially by foreigners. Although

Poland, Romania, and Hungary now permit joint ventures with corporations from outside of the Communist bloc, such arrangements are not common. Much more common is a sharing of the output without a sharing of the ownership: the *buy-back barter* (sometimes called *compensation agreement barter*).

The typical buy-back arrangement involves a company from abroad building a manufacturing or processing facility in a Communist country. The factory would be owned by the local government. The assistance that the private-sector company provides may take forms such as the inflow of equipment, financial capital, patents, technical and managerial assistance, or distribution assistance. In exchange, the contract provides that the company will "buy back" some of the output from the new facility at a reduced price (or even free) as its compensation. For example, Levi Strauss has entered into buy-back barter with Hungary. Part of the "Levis" that will be produced in that country will be sold in Hungary, but the rest will be sold in Western Europe by Levi Strauss. Also, Citroën signed a $370 million contract with East Germany to receive transmissions from a plant that the company is helping to set up for the East German government.

From the viewpoint of the Eastern European host government, this arrangement provides valuable Western assistance without sacrificing control and sometimes with little or no commitment of local capital. Also, continued Western assistance in quality control, technical training, and so on is frequently required.

From the viewpoint of the Western company, this buy-back arrangement can provide access to untapped markets in the Communist world (e.g., many of the contracts involve the company receiving a share of the gross revenues from all sales by the local government as well as from what the company itself sells) and can provide an alternative source of low-cost production for Western markets.

Buy-back barter is also becoming more common outside of the Communist countries, especially with the Organization of Petroleum Exporting Countries (OPEC) and some LDCs.

Switch Trading

The above scenario excludes a type of transaction that some authors list as a separate form of barter: *switch trading*. However, this is not really a separate form of barter but rather the inclusion of a middleman (essentially a broker) who serves to multilateralize the barter arrangement. The "switcher" could be involved in any of the four basic types of barter arrangements listed above. "Switching" is discussed by Barry Westfall in chapter 15.

The above terms and breakdown are somewhat different from most other discussions of barter. The terminology that is used here is designed to avoid ambiguity and to stress the barter nature of the various types of transactions. Exhibit 1.2 summarizes some of the major characteristics of the four varieties.

The four basic forms of barter suggest a variety of approaches that can offer creative financing or creative marketing opportunities to the corporate manager.

EXHIBIT 1.2

THE BASIC CHARACTERISTICS OF THE VARIOUS FORMS OF BARTER

	Number of Contracts	Is Money Used?	Is Credit Extended?	Is Exchange Simultaneous?	Predominance Today
Simple barter = straight barter = pure barter	1*	No	Possibly	Not Necessarily	Relatively Rare**
Parallel barter = counter-purchase barter	2	Yes	Yes	Not Necessarily	Very Common
Clearing-account barter	1	No	Yes	No	Common
Buy-back barter	1	Sometimes	Yes	No	Fairly Common

*either written or oral
**except on the retail level

In addition, other mechanisms have been developed to help make these four types of barter more flexible and easier to use. Whichever barter method is chosen, these tools offer alternatives to traditional monetary exchange—what has been called "the creative non-use of cash."

WHERE BARTER HAS SURVIVED

Barter has always found certain niches of markets in which it has survived—even during the strongest economic booms of modern industrialized economies. However, barter is especially attractive in relatively simple economies or, in more sophisticated economies, in circumstances in which the variety of goods and services is small and the goods are durable and easily transportable. Before the advent of money, all trade was necessarily on a barter basis.

Primitive Markets

Barter predominates in many parts of Latin America, Africa, and Asia, which have never fully entered the modern world (e.g., native markets in many developing countries throughout the world). In those areas, the nonmonetary economy is dominant.

Casual Barter

Another type of barter with a long history is casual barter between friends and associates. This is a portion of even the most modern economies in which, for various reasons, the participants choose to barter instead of use cash. Examples would include the exchange of farm products between farmers, the exchange of dental and medical services between a dentist and physician or even the exchange of babysitting services by mothers in a babysitting co-op. This is all part of the so-called underground economy.

Service Industries

One of the strongest sectors of barter is within certain service industries. For example, the communications media (including television, radio, and magazines) engage extensively in barter. Other major barterers are hotels and airlines. These industries offer a service (for example, advertising time or space, hotel rooms, and airline seats). These services cannot be inventoried: when the television or radio show "airs" or when the journal goes to press or when the hotel "beds down" for the night or when the plane leaves, that ad space, room, or airline seat for that date or flight is lost forever. Accordingly, there is a very strong incentive for the owners of those time or space "slots" to be creative in marketing them by barter.

The marginal cost of the ad space, room, or airline seat is low; therefore, the owners of those slots have shown themselves to be very flexible. Television ad time in exchange for either airline tickets or hotel rooms is a natural pairing; so also is airline tickets in exchange for hotel rooms.

This corporate barter is certainly not limited to exchange of services. For example, television game shows commonly barter for not only the hotel rooms and airline tickets for their contestants but for most or all of the prizes as well. Also, the national television and radio networks commonly provide local stations with free shows in exchange for air time on which the networks can run their ads. The local stations, in turn, receive ready-made programs in which the stations can run *their* ads.

Governmental Policy

Barter has long been a mainstay for Communist countries. For reasons of both politico-economic philosophy and the nature of their economic systems, the currencies of the Communist bloc are generally inconvertible. Those countries often have difficulty in selling to the West. As a result, those countries tend to be short of funds and have a long history of barter.

The Communist governments generally control most domestic production, domestic prices, foreign-exchange rates, and a major share of domestic demand. Market forces play little role. Barter has assumed a dominant role in the trade between Communist-bloc countries in order to (1) facilitate the system of imperative planning within the group, (2) increase their intraregional ties, (3) encourage regional autarky, (4) conserve hard currencies, (5) develop new export markets, (6) dispose of excess production, (7) increase the use of excess capacity, and (8) dispose of low-quality goods that are difficult to sell. The use of bilateral and multilateral barter arrangements has become a formal part of governmental policy. As an example, the Soviet Union exchanges a wide variety of products for Cuban sugar.

These intraregional ties have been weakening in recent years as the individual countries have aggressively sought non-Communist suppliers of industrial equipment and raw materials (e.g., oil). Nevertheless, between countries within the bloc, barter has remained a major vehicle for trade. It has also been increasingly important in trade with non-Communist countries. Bernard Conor addresses the issue of East–West countertrade in chapter 5.

Most Communist governments have carried their proclivity for barter over to their dealings with the LDCs. The rationale of the Communist countries is similar to that which results in barter between the centrally planned countries: the conservation of hard currencies, the establishment of tighter political ties with the bloc, the facilitation of the planning process, and the opportunity to dispose of the excess production or to use excess capacity. Since the Communist country tends to be the stronger country in these relationships with LDCs, it is commonly able to gain acceptance of its preference for barter.

BARTER IN AN AGE OF TURMOIL

The examples of barter that were mentioned above tend to thrive regardless of the strength of the national or world economy. However, in times of economic turmoil, managerial creativity tends to be greatly stimulated—even in the largest, strongest, and most sophisticated industrialized countries. One of the results is greater corporate use of countertrade—barter under many different and imaginative forms.

The 1970s and 1980s

The period since the 1960s has been one of almost chronic economic shock for not only the United States but the entire world. Strains and disruptions have buffeted the world's economies on a scale that has not been seen since the 1930s. This prolonged period of bad economic news has included but has not been limited to:

1. High inflation
2. High interest rates
3. Severe recession
4. Massive unemployment
5. High levels of unutilized productive capacity
6. Widespread bankruptcies
7. High corporate debt
8. High levels of inventories
9. Large governmental budget deficits
10. Severe concern about the safety and security of the banking sector
11. Massive trade imbalances
12. Huge international debts
13. Wild swings in foreign-exchange rates

Countertrade as a Response to Turmoil

Such economic trauma has, not too surprisingly, produced many changes in the economies of the world. A substantial increase in the scale of barter has been one development.

The developing countries: Many of the developing nations of the world have become active promoters of countertrade. They are responding to a variety of motives for bartering: the conservation of hard currency, the disposal of excess production or the use of excess capacity, and the development of new export markets. Not only are many developing countries short of foreign-currency reserves but many have very limited borrowing capacities and very narrow export bases. For example, in much of the developing world, three or fewer products account for 60 percent or more of export receipts. When demand for these products in normal market channels is inadequate, the appeal for barter trade increases. Willis Bussard, in chapter 2, and Christopher McFarlane, in chapter 3, examine these countries.

Also, barter can include elements of foreign aid that are appealing to many developing countries. For example, a five-year barter agreement between Morocco and the USSR permitted Morocco to import heavily in the near term without needing to ship the offsetting bartered goods for several years; this deliberately provided a type of easy-term trade financing to Morocco. Also, the barter ratios can easily be juggled to provide extra "hidden" advantages to the developing countries.

OPEC: Another major impetus for barter has come from the major exporters of oil—especially the members of OPEC. Some of these barter contracts have exceeded $100 million. One of the principal causes of this interest in barter has been a desire to wring greater access to limited supplies of imports such as military equipment and high-technology equipment from foreign suppliers. Thus most of this type of barter has been with the developed countries, not the developing countries. Another appeal of barter for the OPEC countries is that it made cuts in oil prices (when market demand softened) easier to conceal from the other OPEC countries. Algeria, Iran, and Libya have been major price trimmers via barter.

The U.S. Government: Even the United States at times engaged in barter. Agricultural commodities such as wheat, rice, corn, cotton, and tobacco have (when in surplus) been exchanged for goods and services needed abroad by the U.S. military (e.g., repairs for military aircraft) or for goods needed by foreign-aid recipients (such as cement, sugar, and fertilizer).

Nevertheless, the attitude of the U.S. government is somewhat ambivalent. Different agencies often have different views. Congressman Don Bonker (chapter 20), Fred Howell of the Department of Commerce (chapter 21), and Fred Goldberg of the Internal Revenue Service (chapter 19) give several different perspectives for the government. The views of other official institutions are examined by Neil Roger of the World Bank (chapter 22) and Michael Czinkota on the General Agreement on Tariffs and Trade (chapter 23).

THE MODERN RESURGENCE OF BARTER

When Monetary Exchange Suppresses Barter

The use of money tends to prevail over barter systems when conditions are favorable for both the buying and selling companies. Some of these conditions are:

1. An adequate supply of money or credit
2. A monetary unit that is relatively stable in value

3. A strong economy

4. A feeling by both buyers and sellers that they are able to compete successfully and to introduce new products and services

5. Governmental controls that are not felt to be excessive

6. The ability to sell production or inventory before it becomes useless or sharply lower in value

Under these conditions, monetary exchange will generally replace barter. This has generally been true in modern economies—at least since the Great Depression of the 1930s.

The Reemergence of Barter

As we have noted, the period since 1970 has disrupted the conditions listed above. As a result, many individuals, companies, and even countries have found themselves drawn to barter. In the process, they have discovered not only the advantages and the disadvantages of barter but also the modern mechanisms that make the recent burgeoning growth of barter possible.

Industrial corporations: The new barterers are finding that they have good company in the barter business—a virtual who's who of American and world business: Combustion Engineering, Cadbury Schweppes, Northrop, General Foods, AMF, MG, Continental Grain, GM, Ford, Daimler-Benz, VW, General Electric, IBM, Siemens, Krupp, Boeing, McDonnell Douglas, Coca-Cola, Pepsi, Sunkist, and so on are all actively involved in countertrade.

SUMMARY AND CONCLUSIONS

We have now seen that there are four basic varieties of barter or countertrade:

1. Simple, or pure, or straight, or traditional, barter

2. Parallel, or counterpurchase, barter

3. Clearing-account barter

4. Buy-back barter

Parallel barter is the most common variety of wholesale barter today. Simple barter, although very common at the retail level, is the exception on the wholesale level—especially internationally. In most of the following chapters, the terms *barter* and *countertrade* are used interchangeably.

Countertrade is practiced by both corporations and governments. Some governments mandate it; others condemn it. However, many of the governments that condemn barter do permit it and, as in the case of the U.S. government, even practice it themselves.

Countertrade can be bilateral or multilateral. It can involve two products or many. The products can be either goods or services. The exchange of products may be simultaneous or at different times. Money may be used by both parties. Credit may be offered by one or both parties.

Barter has been described as "the creative non-use of cash." It is widely used in primitive markets; between friends or business associates, and in the media and travel industries. It also tends to reappear when the efficiencies of a modern economy break down, typically, during periods of economic trauma: high inflation, interest rates, and unemployment; high levels of inventories, debt, unused productive capacity and bankruptcies; massive trade deficits; wild swings in foreign-exchange rates; and so on. Such conditions have certainly characterized the past decade.

This "creative non-use of cash" has grown rapidly since the early 1970s. This growth is especially prevalent in international trade. The following chapters focus upon international countertrade.

2

An Overview of Countertrade Practices of Corporations and Individual Nations

WILLIS A. BUSSARD

THE PAST DEVELOPMENT OF COUNTERTRADE

Early Countertrade Organizations

One of the earliest international barter organizations was created in 1940 during World War II, in Sweden. That first organization, called SUKAB, was set up by the Ministry of Trade together with export companies in Sweden to combat the growing requirement of countertrade. Right after the war, the Austrians also got very heavily involved in countertrade. Certainly, the Austrians have been prominent players in countertrade ever since. In 1948 Finland made an abortive attempt to institutionalize barter. That organization, called Metex, was simply a combination of metal and electronic industries for the purpose of addressing the developing demands for countertrade.

In 1960 Denmark tried what they called Intercompens, which was an attempt to put together a support system of the Danish companies that were then trying to do countertrading.

Perhaps the most successful group was created in Austria in 1968. The organization, called the Evidence Bureau, still exists in Austria. It is a nonprofit group supported by the Ministry of Foreign Trade, National Chamber of Commerce, and the National Association of Industries. In 1972 they put an office in Bucharest, two years later in Sophia, and in 1976 in Warsaw.

Getting Started with Countertrade

One of the simplest ways for a company to become initiated into countertrade is to accept back something that it would buy back anyway (i.e., simply to shift its source of supply). For example, while I was director of purchasing for the United Fruit Company, we exchanged bananas from our Central American operations for railroad cars from East Germany. It turned out to be one of the best exchanges that United Fruit ever made. Three years ago, when more railroad cars were needed, the company again went to the same East German supplier. It was simply a good buy.

At the time of the first transaction, there were very few countertrade services available. Merban was a name that was on the horizon. There were others that have become publicized since then but that had not yet appeared. For example, Sears World Trade and General Motors Trading had not been created. However, Satra and Phibro had developed and still exist. Amtorg is another survivor; although an American company, it is a subsidiary of the Russian government, which has celebrated its fifty-eighth anniversary in this country.

At that time, in the early 1970s, there was a recognition that there needed to be a better support system for international countertrade. I was involved in an attempt to set up a countertrade cooperative among major companies in the United States. However, the increase of oil prices undercut that effort, and we had to dissolve it. The concept is still good and is being revived again today by other companies.

Unfortunately, the Organization of Petroleum Exporting Countries (OPEC) crisis in 1973–74 certainly spawned many problems that were very different from what we had faced until then—in particular the nonconvertibility of the currencies that were being offered from East Europe.

The demand for countertrade also began expanding in less developed countries at the same time. Offsets, which experienced tremendous growth in the mid–1970s, are examined by Duke Golden in Chapter 7.

SURVEYS OF COUNTERTRADE PRACTICES AND TRENDS

I would like to share with you some of the information that I developed from a countertrade survey of a hundred American companies a little over a year ago. This mail survey evolved from a similar one that I had done in 1973 with the embassies and economic counselors of most trading nations represented either in Washington or in New York. At that time, I was amazed to find that so many countries were requiring, or thinking about, countertrade as a national policy. As a follow-up study, I wanted to ask representative American companies— major industrial companies, exporters, and banks—if what I was told by these embassies really was in effect in the marketplace.

Recent U.S. Government and Canadian Surveys

In preparing our work, we first studied what other research had been done. Four recent surveys were available, two from Canada and two from the U.S. government. Carleton University in Ottawa reported in 1979 on a study of 137

EXHIBIT 2.1

FINDINGS OF PAST COUNTERTRADE SURVEYS

* High technology and capital-project sales require Countertrade (CT)

* Countertrade is increasing:

    * Affects 35% of East-West trade

    * Affects 63% of military sales

    * Affects 10-20% of all world trade in 1980's

* Today CT involves large companies; tomorrow: medium and small

* Serious implications:

    * Transfer of technology

    * Distortion of trade

    * Subsidized competition

* Private sector requires help

export firms; 78 of them had sold goods or services to Eastern Europe, but only 5 had found it necessary to accept Eastern European products in exchange.

A 1981 study by the Canadian Commercial Corporation of nineteen companies that had encountered countertrade demands found that only ten of them actually had to fulfill those commitments.

In 1982 the U.S. International Trade Commission (ITC) ran its first survey. It addressed the issue of the impact of countertrade obligations on U.S. imports. The study concluded that only a small portion of these countertraded goods was actually being brought into the United States. The second ITC study was published in 1985.

The fourth study was done by the U.S. Treasury in 1983. The focus there was upon the offset obligations that had been imposed upon twenty-six U.S. aerospace firms. The study concluded that the offset demands were substantial— $16.1 billion of sales had led to $9.5 billion of offset obligations. These conclusions certainly support Duke Golden's comments in chapter 7.

Our conclusions from these four surveys were that in recent years countertrade in North America could be characterized (see Exhibit 2.1) as:

1. A technique being applied primarily to large capital projects and hi-tech products (e.g., 63 percent of military sales)

2. Very important in East–West trade (35 percent of all East–West trade)

3. On the increase for large companies but now beginning to involve exporters of all sizes

4. Significantly altering traditional trading patterns

5. Not yet developed, either in Canada or the United States, a clearly defined focal point or organization for helping private companies deal together with this growing problem

All of the surveys indicated a sharply increasing requirement for countertrade in the sale of military hardware to developed country governments or large aircraft to national airlines.

The results of these surveys must be used carefully. One result particularly is often misquoted. Note that countertrade affects 35 percent of East–West trade—not 35 percent of world trade. Some 10 to 20 percent of all world trade is a reasonable and conservative figure for how important countertrade is today in the mid–1980s. It is increasing, but I cannot tell you what it is going to be by 1990.

The Countertrade Project Survey

The four previous studies answered many questions and helped to raise the level of awareness of many corporate managers and government officials. However, there were still many unanswered questions. We addressed many of these in our own survey. Among the issues raised were:

1. How rapidly is countertrade increasing in international trade?

2. What has been the impact upon U.S. exports?

3. Can countertrade be managed?

4. How do other countries handle the problem of countertrade demands by importing countries?

5. What do companies expect future trends to be?

To answer these issues, we sent a four-page survey to a selected group of firms in the United States. Useful responses were received from 110 firms plus 12 commercial banks. Excluded from consideration were two specialized varieties of barter: (1) those goods that were exchanged under government-to-government bilateral trade treaties and (2) like-type commodities exchanged by oil and other companies for their own convenience or to reduce unnecessary transportation.

Countries involved in countertrade: In 1972 only about fifteen countries were involved in countertrade. Because most of them were East European countries or other nonmarket economies, it was more familiarly known at that time as a variety of East–West trade. However, several developed countries such as Australia and New Zealand were among these fifteen. The U.S. government was also countertrading at that time through its Commodity Credit Corporation (CCC). Excess agricultural products were bartered for materials for the strategic stockpile.

Seven years later, by 1979, twelve more countries were requesting countertrade arrangements. Most were in South America and the Mid-East; they were buying defense equipment under offset programs. However, some highly industrialized countries could also be included in this group. The sale of Northrop F–5's to Switzerland in 1975 under the Federal Military Sales program was one example of the growth of offsets during this period. Since that time, Northrop has helped market more than $300 million of Swiss products throughout the world as part of its countertrade obligations.

Today, according to the survey respondents in 1984, there are more than eighty-eight countries that request some form of countertrade arrangement before they agree to buy U.S. exports. This large increase within just four years represents many less developed as well as developing countries that find themselves with large debts. Unable to devote funds needed for interest or principal repayments to trade, they can acquire necessary imports only by trading native products.

More than 55 percent of the major trading nations of the world have resorted to some form of countertrading.

Rate of increase in countertrade: The annual growth in the number of countertrade transactions in recent years, which were reported by survey respondents, correlated closely with the growing number of countries involved. The number of total transactions reported in 1981 was 50 percent greater than that which the same companies experienced in 1980.

In 1982 the total countertrade transactions reported by the same companies was 64 percent greater than that experienced in 1981. For some companies, 1982 offered as high as a 200 percent increase in countertrade transactions. The year 1983 was a high point with an overall average growth in countertrade transactions of 117 percent within one year.

Prevalent forms of countertrade: The survey respondents reported (Exhibit 2.2) that counterpurchase is the primary type of countertrade being used (55 percent); indeed, it exceeds the total of all other types of countertrade combined. Traditional barter is not used often. Switch trading was used less than buy-back. Offset is the second most common form of countertrade.

Industries in which countertrade is required: Countertrade is now required in the sale of a wide variety of products by U.S. producers (Exhibit 2.3). Sellers of heavy industrial equipment, (e.g., construction, heavy trucks, and large farm equipment) found the greatest need to respond to countertrade requests to consummate their sales (23 percent of the total). Manufactured goods, oil-field goods, and aerospace products together accounted for an additional third of the reported countertrade transactions during the past four years. In total, all companies involved in any kind of countertrade reported that an average of 4 percent of all exports required a countertrade arrangement.

EXHIBIT 2.2

COUNTERTRADE USAGE-By Types

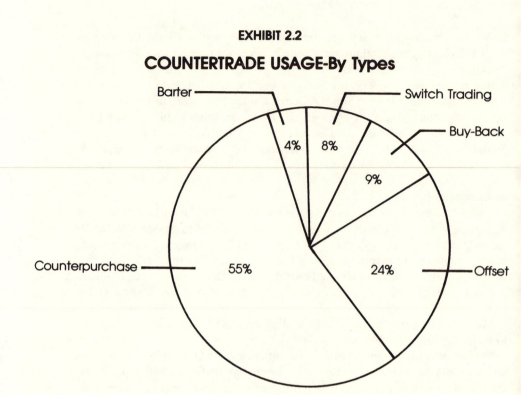

- Barter — 4%
- Switch Trading — 8%
- Buy-Back — 9%
- Counterpurchase — 55%
- Offset — 24%

EXHIBIT 2.3

INDUSTRIES INVOLVED IN U.S. COUNTERTRADE

23%	Industrial Development	4%	Computers
11%	Manufactured Goods	4%	Electronics
11%	Oil-Field Goods	4%	Health Care
11%	Aerospace	4%	Tobacco
9%	Chemicals	2%	Photographic
6%	Food	2%	Military Spares
4%	Construction Projects	2%	Services
4%	Pharmaceuticals		

However, when those companies dealing with countertrade as an everyday facet of their export sales were evaluated as a separate group, it was found that countertrade affected 8 percent of their exports. Individual companies in several industries reported much higher percentages:

Aerospace	47 percent
Construction	27 percent
Electronics and defense	20 percent
Chemicals and minerals	15 percent

Sales lost: One of the questions asked in the survey was: how many sales failed because of your inability or unwillingness to arrange a satisfactory countertrade agreement? The aggregate answer was 5 percent, based on total export sales. For all companies answering this question, this represented forty-five lost sales worth $380 million. For one company alone it represented $45 million in lost sales.

It was significant to note, in terms of ability to prevent lost sales, that of those companies that had established their own trading subsidiary, not one reported any lost sales.

Length of negotiating period: One of the standard criticisms of countertrade is the long negotiation period. The respondents verified this. Of the companies, 46 percent said that it takes one to six months to negotiate a countertrade deal. Another 30 percent said that it took six to twelve months, and about a quarter of them said that it takes over a year.

Proportion of countertrade demanded by countries: Another important question related to the amount of compensation that countries require. As is shown in Exhibit 2.4, 50 to 100 percent is the most common requirement. However, Peru and Jamaica were listed a number of times as asking more than 100 percent. The Bombadier Company has been cited as offering a 300 percent compensation to get a deal on some weapons and military vehicles. (The English are protesting because they wanted to give only 200 percent.) Countertrade is definitely getting to be a marketing requirement if you are going after the high-dollar contracts.

Costs of disposal of countertrade goods: The costs of disposing of countertrade goods are twofold: (1) the commission paid to outsiders for their assistance and (2) the discount necessary to accept for the countertrade goods in finally disposing of them.

Of the respondents, 67 percent reported paying commissions to outsiders of 2 to 5 percent. However, 17 percent paid 1 percent or less while an equal proportion paid more than 5 percent.

Discounts required for final disposition of the goods averaged 12 percent. However, 29 percent of the respondents paid 5 percent or less, and 28 percent paid 15 percent or more.

When the U.S. exporters were asked if they were able to include their costs

EXHIBIT 2.4

COMPENSATION REQUIRED

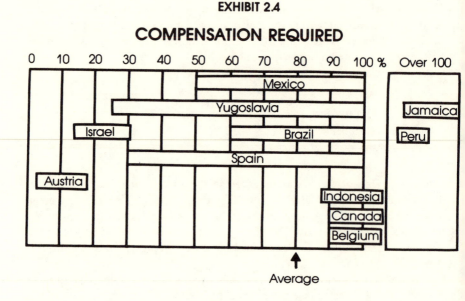

Average

of disposing of countertrade goods in their sales price, almost one-half said yes. However, one-third reported recovering only part of their disposition costs; 18 percent reported recovering none of their disposition costs in their sales price.

Using countertrade specialists: It is a very common practice for companies to use specialists to help facilitate countertrade (Exhibit 2.5). Of firms surveyed, 30 percent relied primarily upon in-house specialists or trading subsidiaries. However, trading houses both here and abroad were used in 44 percent of the cases. International banks furnished these same services in 20 percent of the cases. Foreign-government agencies, brokers, and consultants accounted for the remainder of the outside services used by the reporting companies. More than half (53 percent) of the countertrading companies reported using more than one type of specialist.

Disposition of countertrade goods: One critical point in agreeing to accept countertrade goods is to determine where to dispose of them (Exhibit 2.6). Of the companies responding, the largest number (45 percent) were able to absorb the goods within their own division, subsidiaries, or affiliates. Eight percent received assistance from their suppliers. The balance turned responsibility over to trading companies, barter agents, or banks.

Regardless of who handled the disposition, almost three-fourths of the countertraded goods were consumed outside of the United States. This confirmed the results of the first U.S. ITC study. Only 28 percent of the goods were imported to the United States.

Future of countertrade: Almost everyone surveyed said that countertrade is

EXHIBIT 2.5

COUNTERTRADE SERVICES EMPLOYED

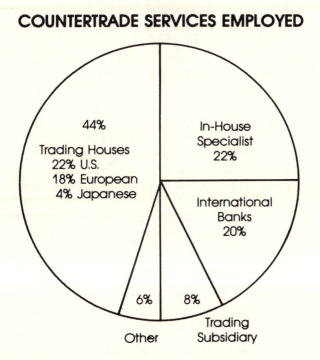

44%
Trading Houses
22% U.S.
18% European
4% Japanese

In-House
Specialist
22%

International
Banks
20%

6%
Other

8%
Trading
Subsidiary

EXHIBIT 2.6

DISPOSITION OF COUNTERTRADE GOODS

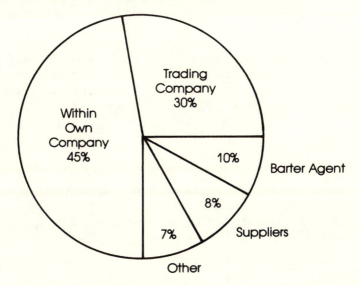

Trading
Company
30%

Within
Own
Company
45%

10%
Barter Agent

8%
Suppliers

7%
Other

going to persist as a factor in international trade. Some of the reasons given were the continuing debt problem and shortage of foreign exchange, general world economic conditions, the need to transfer technology, and economic-development needs.

To respond to this scenario, 76 percent of the companies said they would use a U.S. trading company to dispose of goods in the future. This is substantially different from the responses to the questions of what the companies have done in the past (Exhibit 2.5). The proportion of international banks to be used was also much bigger this time. The banks are also setting up their own trading companies to service their clients. James Barkas (chapter 9) and Christopher McFarlane (chapter 3) address that issue.

The Cooperative Exchange, which a group of companies had unsuccessfully tried to initiate in the early 1970s, is still a possible way to build up a support system for U.S. companies. Also, 23 percent of the respondents said that their companies would probably create their own trading subsidiaries. However, as Stephen Crain discusses in chapter 8, such efforts will not always be successful.

COUNTERTRADE PRACTICES OF INDIVIDUAL NATIONS

Sweden

The Swedish efforts are private sector. SUKAB, which was mentioned as an early Swedish effort, still exists. In addition, ASEA, the international electronic company, has set up its own trading company in Switzerland with offices around the world. Also, Axel Johnson joined with the Wallenberg Group to create a new company called Mercator in order to address the countertrade issues that have to be considered by Swedish companies.

Japan

Five major Japanese trading companies have facilities in New York. All stress that they intend to become predominant and preeminent in the field of counter-trade. This is one of their objectives for the coming years. They are definitely not overlooking countertrade but see it as a growing trend and something they need to address.

Austria

We have already discussed some of the Austrian activities. In addition, the Centro Bank of Austria was created as a combination of about six major national banks. They have the window into East Europe through Bank Handlowi in Warsaw.

Netherlands

The Dutch, through the Rotterdam Chamber of Commerce, have just created their own effort in countertrade, trying to pull together something that will aid all of the Dutch companies.

Belgium

The Belgian company, SOCSER, has seen a need to address countertrade as a separate issue from the rest of international trade. SOCSER has set up a new company called General Trade Support. In addition, the Office of Foreign Trade in Belgium is now setting up its own advisory service for the rest of Belgian export and import companies.

United Kingdom

The United Kingdom has recently put out a very good brochure called the "Countertrade Guide to Exporters," indicating that its government, through many systems, agencies, and departments, is going to offer the same kind of support to its companies that friends on the continent are offering. In addition, a countertrade data base, called Batis, has been created in London.

France

ACECO, an association of companies involved in countertrade, was started in 1977 by five of the major banks, the government, and a number of the major industries in France. It put together a support system to help the French companies compete and currently has 17 major banks supporting it. Its major activities are, first, information collection and sharing among its 150 companies and bank outlets and, second, counseling any French company that faces a countertrade problem overseas. It tries to prepare those companies before they go overseas as to what the implications and problems could be. This French group is very successful; it could serve as a model for a similar support system in the United States.

A PROPOSAL FOR AN AMERICAN RESPONSE

I have been involved in organizing a new group of organizations in the United States that are interested in international countertrade. We are exploring the development of a response in this country to some of the trends in the above-mentioned countries.

The group, Countertrade Coalition, comprises eleven international trade associations in the United States including the China Trade Council and the National Foreign Trade Council. We are trying to find out what U.S. industry really needs to do to compete overseas with companies that have the kinds of support system from their governments or industry groups that were described above.

We have identified several tentative objectives. First, we need a single focal point in the United States for coordinating all kinds of countertrade efforts so that we know who is presenting a seminar such as the one upon which this book is based and even to help define the basic terms of our industry (e.g., we still have had several different interpretations of one concept such as offset). Second, we lack a data base of all essential up-to-date countertrade information. Before company marketing managers go overseas, they need to know exactly what they are going to be faced with, what regulations changed yesterday, how many items that were offered in Indonesia are not being offered today, and so on. All of these things need to be known before a countertrade offer can be structured.

Several companies, including Northrop and General Electric, are creating their own data bases. However, for different companies to do this separately is wasteful, expensive, and not available to all. What is needed is a joint effort such as the aforementioned Batis in London.

The third thing that should be considered is the creation of an umbrella organization, a center for alternative trade. Perhaps it could be created at the University of South Carolina or some other university. Its focus should be to encompass everything that is discussed in this book—not just countertrade and counterpurchase but the whole area of enhancing the ability of U.S. exporters to send their goods overseas. It would also be a logical location for the data base.

There are many ways that we can help U.S. industry combat competition resulting from countertrade efforts by foreign companies. My hope is that by knowing this and by setting up this kind of facility, we can then help develop a strategic plan for our own companies and for our government. In this way we can hope to learn how to live creatively with this obligation to take back something in certain trade, equity investments, or whatever it is, to keep our exports going. With a $140 billion trade deficit, we have to consider the need for a strategic plan.

You may think I am painting a very pessimistic picture. However, I do not intend that because, from my own experience, I am very encouraged by things that have happened in the past year or two. Three years ago, I was very discouraged, but today there are many things underway that will help the situation. The new International Trade Commission survey is a thirty-page document sent to 580 companies. The answers that are coming back are very minute in detail. It is an attempt by the government to learn how serious this countertrade problem is and to try to define the issues that we have to address as a group.

In terms of the data bases, three things that are happening are very encouraging. As was noted, some major companies are setting up their own data bases. However, that does not help the medium-size company or the small company that still needs to countertrade. Whether a company is big or small, if it sells something overseas, it needs a source for the answer to its problems.

The directories of the International Trade and Marketing Associates (ITMA) in Minneapolis was a second development; however, it is not available on-line but is available as a printed publication. The third effort is called the Trade Tech Exchange; it is a very complete approach to setting up a data base from which one can pick out exactly what one needs to know. It will be on the General Electric Information Services Company (GEISCO) network in about fifty-one countries.

CONCLUSIONS

There are several points to bear in mind. First, countertrade is increasing: it is encouraged by some companies and endured by others. Whether you find countertrade to be an opportunity to develop new business or an added difficulty to be surmounted, it is not going to go away. We have to learn to live with it. Second, other nations have developed better and more consistent approaches to helping each individual company in their countries to compete. It is time that the United States begins to take a better look at countertrade and to create some sort of competitive program that will help reduce the $140 billion trade deficit.

PART II

COUNTERTRADE PRACTICES IN DIFFERENT REGIONS OF THE WORLD

3

Countertrade in Latin America and the Caribbean

CHRISTOPHER D. McFARLANE

Manufacturers Hanover Trust has been involved in countertrade for about two and one-half years. Our involvement in countertrade focuses upon trying to solve financial problems of our clients with marketing solutions. Our client base includes companies that either cannot get paid or cannot get the necessary import licenses. With that kind of criteria, our emphasis has been on Latin America.

Our countertrade unit is composed of four people in New York and one in London. The emphasis is here in New York because we are concentrating mainly on Latin America. In contrast to Eastern Europe, countertrade in Latin America is not yet well institutionalized.

Countertrade in Latin America and most other developing areas is primarily a result of the debt crisis. There are some good thoughts about export promotion and development of new export markets, but if there had not been a major debt problem, there would probably be little countertrade in Latin America. Countertrade is not a fundamental solution to some of the longer-term debt problems in Latin America, but it may be an intermediate step and it may have some benefit.

It is important to recognize that trade policy is generally subordinated to financial policy in a period of a major debt crisis, and countertrade is a relatively small part of that overall trade policy. It is not easy to negotiate a countertrade deal for $2 million worth of computers in Brazil if its major concern right then is signing a $5 billion rescheduling loan. However, we are over the initial hurdle of reschedulings. It is now a little easier to institutionalize the mechanisms for countertrade in various countries. Certain Latin countries have already issued clear-cut, relatively straightforward regulations. Some countries are considering them. Other countries have basically chosen to turn their backs on the entire issue.

MEXICO

A good example would be Mexico. It highlights the problems that a private-sector company can have in trying to countertrade. About two years ago, the Mexican government at the peak of its debt crisis said that it was in favor of some kind of a countertrade. It published an official decree authorizing the sale of "comprabantes," which were receipts given to exporters. The comprabantes could be used as a type of import entitlement. If a company in Mexico exported $10 worth of goods and needed only $5 worth of imports, it could sell the additional $5 worth of receipts (comprabantes) to another authorized importer.

The sale would have to go through a special governmental body that was created to monitor the countertrade program and to insure that incremental exports were being generated and that the imports were essential. The problem was that the body consisted of four governmental ministries—the Ministry of Finance, the Central Bank, the Ministry of Trade, and the Trade Promotion Board. Trying to get one agency, let alone four, to agree on what was an incremental export was virtually impossible.

In general, the comprabante program did not work as the government had expected. There were very strong pockets of resistance in each of the different agencies. The comprabantes probably were a forerunner of the international trade certificates that Paul Boliek discusses in chapter 13—the exporter had the right to sell to an importer. That was a great theory. Unfortunately, because of all of the bureaucracy, it did not get very far. However, what did occur shows how countertrade can help importers to cope.

Under Mexican regulations, there was a dual exchange rate put into effect during the time of the crisis, which was the summer of 1983. There was about a 14 percent differential between the controlled market rate at which you exported and the free-market rate that was applied to imports.

Another quirk in Mexican foreign-exchange regulations allows foreign exchange that is earned from exports to stay outside the country for sixty or ninety days, depending on the particular official approval process. As a result of these inconsistencies, some strange arbitrage transactions occurred. For example, a major computer company bought Mexican tomato paste to export. This was done as a means to generate foreign exchange (at the controlled rate). Those dollar funds were used to pay for the import of computers. The Mexican exporter and the U.S. importer already had a contract or at least an understanding. In this case, the computer company would purchase the tomato paste locally, in pesos. The cost would be 5 percent to "buy" the export, but they would be the exporter of record and could put that in their bank account outside of Mexico for sixty or ninety days. During those sixty or ninety days, any imports could be financed from those funds held in the account. What happened was that although the company lost 5 percent on the sale of the tomato paste, it gained 14 percent because it was able to use the proceeds from the sale of the tomato paste, which was at the more favorable controlled exchange rate, to finance the imports.

This kind of process was going on much more frequently and regularly than any kind of a comprabante sale, and it highlighted two concepts. First, the individual who is the most clever is the one who has the biggest problem, and that is going to be the importer—not the government. Second, this example highlights the problems in creating structures for countertrade. Mexico abandoned the need for this kind of arbitrage system: imports now can generally use the same exchange rate as exports, so the opportunity for arbitrage has disappeared. What Mexico has done instead is to target individual industries and say, ''Look, if you're in the automotive area and you import, you must export a certain percentage of that.'' The government applies this policy industry by industry.

ECUADOR

A second example of a country that has a countertrade policy in effect is Ecuador. The policy has been in effect for more than a year in its current form, although it had been around for a couple of years before that with different requirements. It is the longest standing policy of any in the Latin American countries. Ecuador is a good case study because its structure is essentially the same as the one being used in Colombia today and also the one being considered by Argentina and Brazil. If you understand the countertrade policies of Ecuador, you will understand much of Latin America.

As it currently stands, an importer in Ecuador makes its application to MECEI, the trade ministry, which is the government office that must approve a barter contract. The company must present two applications—one for import and one for export. Once approval is gained from MECEI, the contract must be registered with the Central Bank. Traditionally, one of the big problems in Ecuador has been the time factor. For a while last year, the government switched the approval process from MECEI to the Central Bank. It then found that everybody continued to think that the trade ministry was still involved. This caused a traffic jam of applications that just lengthened the time factor. It has now gone back to MECEI and been streamlined, so that a barter contract can be approved within a relatively short time provided a company is persistent.

The normal structure of the contract is just what you would think. First the exports are generated. Funds are placed in an escrow account when the importer in the United States pays for the goods. At that point the important part is to consider what is going on in Ecuador. The Ecuadorian importer, who is the partner in the barter contract, will then make a payment to the exporter in the local currency (sucres). At the same time, the export documents are presented to indicate that the U.S. importer of the Ecuadorian product (for example, tuna) has made payment in dollars. The dollar funds are placed in an escrow account with Manufacturers Hanover. Simultaneous transactions occur in the local and overseas markets, and at that time Manufacturers Hanover issues an indemnity stating that within 180 days any dollar funds remaining in this account will be remitted back to Ecuador. The only exception to that would be that goods exported from the United States can be paid for just like a normal letter of credit.

Thus tuna sales might be going out from Ecuador and pharmaceuticals might be coming in. When the U.S. exporter, the pharmaceutical company, presents its documents, we will pay them from the dollar proceeds in the escrow account; then we will notify the Ecuadorian Central Bank that our indemnity is diminished by the amount of the sale. That is generally the basic structure in a number of countries.

For a tuna exporter, this type of barter deal enables him to get his money up front. The U.S. exporter of pharmaceuticals has a guarantee of payment; for exports to Ecuador, prompt payment can be a concern. However, under this system, the exporter knows that the money is on deposit with a fine institution outside the country. Default is not usually the worry. The issue is time—the U.S. exporter naturally wants the benefit of having the funds available as soon as the goods are shipped.

However, and this is also important, the Ecuadorian importer appears to be the one who is stuck with the bill. He paid the Ecuadorian exporter of tuna when the export receipts in dollars were escrowed—not when the importer received the goods. However, even for the Ecuadorian importer, there are advantages to that. First, in Ecuador there is a sliding devaluation; by paying now the importer can fix his local-currency cost today rather than wait a mandatory four months. He knows his dollar cost, and he can use today's exchange rate to make the payment—that saves him money. It is true that the importer does have to prepay for the goods in a sense. He may have to wait as long as six months sometimes to get the goods, and he is prefinancing the import, but he saves the cost of the devaluation of the sucre. That is the basic formalized system that is used in Latin America today.

COLOMBIA

Colombia is probably the hottest market for countertrade in Latin America today. However, the countertrade program there is not being applied as sensibly as it might be. It is a little heavy-handed. There are basically too few export goods being chased by too many exporters. As a result, the cost of the countertrade today can range as high as 30 percent. The Colombian government has basically said that all importers in nonessential industries, which they define fairly broadly, must countertrade if they want to get their import licenses. It is very difficult in a relatively small economy like Colombia to implement that kind of a mandate without any forewarning. There simply is not enough readily recognizable exports from Colombia today to facilitate the demand by the importers. As a result, they are bidding up the price of the appropriate exports. In turn, the costs of the imported goods are being raised to compensate for the extra cost of the countertrade exports.

The structure of barter in Colombia is basically the same as in Ecuador. The ruling body is Incomex. The importer again sponsors the application and what is called a SEIC contract. The original thought in Colombia was that a company would sponsor an export to get credit for an import. The exporter would not use the actual funds generated by the export to finance its import. Instead, it would get the credit that would allow the company to get its import permit. Because of the deteriorating situation in Colombia, external escrow accounts are used. Incomex is willing to permit this so that a company does not get caught in any kind of financial rescheduling.

The Colombian system has changed from simply a credit mechanism to more of a barter-type procedure. One peculiarity in Colombia is that the import can occur before the export of another good is required. This is done on an approval basis where there is merely a timing-gap difference. Both contracts must be carefully spelled out. IBM for example could not offer to bring in its computers and guarantee to export a corresponding amount within six months. The parallel-barter proposal must be specific. For example, IBM might say, "We will export cotton in six months, but because it has not been harvested yet, we cannot deliver until then." The company must give to Incomex an indemnity that has a penalty clause. Basically, in Colombia today, the program is very much the same as it is in Ecuador in terms of structure, and the problem right now is simply finding appropriate exports.

BRAZIL

Brazil maintains its traditional policy of reviewing barter proposals on a case-by-case basis. The Brazilian government says that, as a general rule, it is not in favor of countertrade as an acceptable means of financing trade. However, on an exceptional basis, it will permit barter transactions.

Brazil encourages major importers to generate exports, and that has become fairly big business—building export programs. This can take on a lot of different forms. There are companies that have set up their own trading companies in Brazil to export completely nontraditional products. For example, although an automotive company may be involved in the import of automative goods, it may export wood first. When it goes to Cacex, the regulatory body in Brazil, it simply says, "Look, we're generating Brazilian exports; please give us some credit so we can import more." Cacex is generally receptive to that approach.

Any major multinational that has an assembly plant or a major sales operation in Brazil should consider starting some kind of export operation. One hopes it could be in the organization's own product line, but it might consider other products as well. How one does that is a case-by-case decision. For example, one major chemical company is purchasing a substantial amount of goods from Brazil. Its Brazilian affiliate is not the exporter of record. Yet it approaches

Cacex every year and says, "My parent company bought $40 million worth of exports from Brazil; now please give us credit for that." In that particular case, Cacex agreed. But one of the dominant features about Brazil is the fact that it very much involves case-by-case approval. What this company can do, another company might request but might be turned down. Furthermore, the rationale might never be clearly understood.

The most obvious source of "traditional" countertrade in Brazil is the switch trading (or clearing). Barry Westfall discusses switching in chapter 15. Switching is the major form of countertrade in Brazil—particularly the East German and the Hungarian clearings, mainly because both East Germany and Hungary have credit facilities and a very shrewd perception of what can and cannot be done in Brazil.

Additional bilateral clearing agreements in Brazil are unlikely. One central bank employee said that it was a long-stated policy of the government not to increase pure bilateral trading agreements. Petrobras, the national oil company, however, has been very clever in the use of its purchasing power. The company has made it a national priority to use its purchasing with those countries from whom Brazil buys goods to promote Brazilian exports. For example, there is a major barter deal between Brazil and Iraq that basically involves chickens in exchange for oil. There are also manufactured goods sent to Nigeria in exchange for oil. In both cases Petrobras, not the government, made the deal happen. I am impressed at how cleverly it has manipulated its buying power.

Petrobras, when it lets out bids, will sometimes ask the seller to consider an offset program to purchase goods through Petrobras' trading company, Interbras. Petrobras is a "big brother" helping Interbras stay above water. A company that is bidding on sales to Petrobras will likely encounter a request to consider some kind of an offset program through Interbras. The one good thing about that is that almost anything can be bought from Interbras because it is a general trading company. The problem is that you could probably get the same products more cheaply if you went directly to the producer in Brazil.

ARGENTINA

It is likely that Argentina will begin a countertrade program in the relatively near future. There have been administrative decrees modeled after the Colombian and Ecuadorian type of rules. Basically, because the old government was against countertrade, the new government will likely be in favor of countertrade. This should open up some interesting opportunities because Argentina is a much broader-based economy than either Ecuador or Colombia. One hopes it will learn by some of Colombia's problems and perhaps enact the legislation more carefully.

CENTRAL AMERICA

Central America is very much a case-by-case situation. If a company has a good import deal and it can find a product to export, it is possible—in almost any of the countries in Central America—to do it on a barter basis. There is little institutionalization of barter in Central America, although Costa Rica and Guatemala have issued decrees saying that countertrade is permitted—provided that nontraditional export goods are involved.

THE CARIBBEAN

The major problem that the Caribbean area has today is the breakdown in regional trade. That is primarily because Guyana owes everybody money, and the Caribbean area is low on the list of countries it plans to pay. As a result, there is a great deal of trade friction intraregionally. That will probably be eased somewhat with the new prime minister in Barbados. Relations will likely improve with Trinidad, the economic super power for that area.

Jamaica is the one country where countertrade might be readily considered by the government. The biggest problem is that Jamaica does not have very much for which there is a strong foreign market. There is not much prospect of the government being interested in listening to an aluminum or bauxite proposal at the depressed prices in today's market. Tourism actually is a workable deal in Jamaica today. Occupancy rates in hotels are off because of the riots the country suffered in February 1985. If a foreign company had a high priority export to Jamaica and said it would take payment in tourism, the government would probably be amenable to that kind of proposal. However, be prepared for some very long and difficult negotiations.

ALADI

Aladi is the Latin American regional payment mechanism. Particularly for larger companies, Aladi can be used for sourcing from one Latin American country and making sales to another Latin American country. Some companies have been able to get around serious payment problems by just changing the source of supply. Aladi works basically as a bilateral clearing house. There is a central headquarters in Lima. Each country maintains with all of the other countries in Latin America a running balance of its exports and imports. The exporter gets paid in its local currency. The importer pays in its local currency. Once every quarter the central banks settle up the debt owed between the two countries. The effect for a foreign company is that, if it can source out of Argentina when it makes a sale to Brazil, it may get the local currency payment much more quickly than if dollars were required. But there can be problems if a company hopes to import raw materials in order to produce the goods in Argentina to sell to Brazil.

4

Countertrade in Western Europe

KATE MORTIMER

N. M. Rothschild & Sons is a very old merchant bank. Merchant banks are not lending banks in the sense that Bank of America or Chase Manhattan are, but much of what lending we do is trade related and much of our fee-earning business is international. In the case of Rothschilds, there is the additional relevant feature of our role in the international gold market. This does not involve just gold contracts (futures and so on) but also the physical trading of gold in large quantities. Rothschilds acts both as principal and as agent in gold trading. Therefore we are, as far as precious metals go, a genuine trading company as well as a bank, complete with "traffic" department and storage capacity.

In addition, we owned until recently a share in a Hong Kong-based trading company specializing in the China trade; we intend shortly to set up another. In Europe, we have a Swiss subsidiary in Zurich called Creafin, which specializes in "à forfait" (essentially a form of buying receivables at a discount) and other forms of lending to "difficult" (i.e., high margin) credits. Opportunities for extending our work to countertrade (or the requirement to do so) come naturally and the location in Switzerland and the nature of previous lending business provides good access to trading-company counterparties.

HISTORICAL PERSPECTIVE

The monetized economy has been the exception rather than the rule for most of the world until as recently as the nineteenth century. The French historian Braudel in *Civilisation Materielle et Capitalisme* recounted, in his history of the ordinary person from the fifteenth to the nineteenth centuries, how rare were genuine financial transactions—as opposed to barter in various forms. Even the use of gold, silver, and copper as money was more akin to barter than to money payment as we know it or knew it during the periods of fixed exchange rates in the twentieth century. Transport problems prevented effective arbitrage between countries with differing incidence of precious metal supplies, and the value of gold varied from place to place as well as over time.

Coming into more modern times, European banks have continued to make a large part of their business the financing of international trade: by discounting bills (in London and in the à forfait market), by lending directly to traders on the security of the goods consigned, and by raising syndicated or other export credits, with or without the guarantee of official export-insurance agencies. Lending on the security of goods being traded inherently bears the risk that the bank may have to take the goods and dispose of them, and this risk has been realized from time to time.

Finally, in this brief historical overview, two twentieth-century upheavals caused numerous unorthodox, countertradelike trading methods. First, the post–World War I hyperinflation in Germany rendered money virtually useless in trade with that country. Second, after World War II there were initially bilateral clearing agreements between the European states and then the European Payments Union. The latter was a multilateral clearing arrangement that lasted from 1948 to 1958. Throughout the years the provision for settlement of balances in gold or dollars was gradually increased until 75 percent of trade was being settled financially and the union was dissolved.

I think this explains why, for Europeans, as perhaps also for the Japanese, countertrade, as we now understand it, is only a variation on a long-running theme binding finance to trade.

THE APPROACH OF EUROPEAN BANKS TO COUNTERTRADE

Merchant Banks

Generally, with a few exceptions, merchant banks—indeed, most European banks—are not wildly enthusiastic about countertrade and get involved only because they believe they must. For merchant banks, client pressure is the main incentive, so those banks with important clients that are big exporters or that specialize in project finance have had to learn about countertrade.

The field is divided between those banks that have invested in trading companies, to whom they pass their clients' countertrade business, and those who treat countertrade as part of their general "financial engineering" repertoire. The first group includes notably Kleinwort Benson and some continental banks; the activities of their associated trading companies were, and still are largely, directed at East–West trade.

The second group is more numerous but includes banks that have in fact done little or no countertrade business because no serious opportunity has arisen or has been forced on them. Typically, a merchant bank would get involved through a major piece of export-credit business (e.g., to Indonesia) or through a project financing. In Rothschilds' case, our bullion dealing also provides an entree.

Our imports of gold or silver bullion from Third World countries are a natural target for British exporters wanting a countertrade credit with the exporting country. Our interests lie with our client, the foreign bullion exporter. We will advise him or his government if the government wishes its sales to us to be part of a countertrade deal.

As you can imagine, this does not happen very often since bullion is a highly tradeable cash commodity of the sort that less developed countries (LDCs) usually wish to exclude from their countertrade programs. There is more demand for gold or silver loans as an element in the financing of new mines or mine extensions, but this is akin to countertrade only in that both sides of the deal are denominated in a commodity rather than in cash.

Project finance: Merchant banks are beginning to find that, even outside the Soviet bloc, countertrade is impinging on project finance. For some of us, very much including Rothschild, arranging project finance is a key fee-earning activity, so it is in this sphere that we are most likely to respond to the demand for countertrade skills. They are beginning to be part of the standard range of skills required in financial engineering.

Countertrade arises in project financing in two ways: first, through the now relatively well-known mechanism of buy-back agreements, which were described by Christopher Korth in chapter 1. As you know, they sound much more straightforward than they are. The time profile of such deals poses many problems that the financial adviser has to handle in concert with his legal partners. But the risks involved are essentially the same as those in nonrecourse project financings, which a merchant bank regularly designs and helps to negotiate. If the output of the project is late, smaller than expected, of lower quality or simply less valuable than expected, the lender whose only recourse is to the project is in trouble in the same way whether he calculated and arranged repayment in goods or in the cash that the goods would generate. Countertrade of this sort is therefore an aspect of the risk-evaluating and risk-splitting skill that a good project-finance specialist must have.

A new type of countertrade angle to project finance is emerging as a result of the debt crisis. Projects, which may be economically justifiable in their own right but do not themselves generate foreign exchange (or exportable goods), are becoming increasingly hard to finance, especially in heavily indebted countries. Lenders no longer want a generalized country risk. It is logical to expect that people will try to solve this problem by tying in exports of other goods from the country in question to provide the necessary stream of foreign exchange as security for project lenders. This may not make good economic sense, and it may even contravene the spirit if not the letter of negative-pledge clauses in World Bank and other loan agreements. However, it is still likely to be tried and, indeed, is being tried.

Merchant banks, like most commercial banks, will not take the countertrade goods onto their own books (except the few like Kleinwort Benson and Midland, which have trading subsidiaries or associate companies). As mentioned earlier, Rothschilds has had a trading company in the Far East and will have another, but this is for commission -or agency business not trading as principal, or not usually, and not particularly associated with countertrade. Most merchant banks regard their role to be that of introducers, finance raisers, risk definers and allocators, negotiators, and documentation organizers. They will also perform the same role for exporters who are operating outside the confines of a project, but most of that business tends to go to commercial banks that are more willing to put up the necessary credit as well. In addition, merchant banks are extremely keen to act as cash managers for the large amounts of money that have to be put in escrow, sometimes for long periods, as part of a countertrade deal. One or two British merchant banks are also looking for a role advising Third World governments on their countertrade policies and regarding particular transactions.

Commercial Banks

Most European commercial banks have made some attempt to organize themselves for countertrade. On the Continent the norm is either to invest in a portion of a trading company or to designate the à-forfait dealers as countertrade referral points. Although the business is not the same, the clients often are and à-forfait dealers often know the players in the commodity markets better than other bank staff do. Similarly, in Britain, the big banks put their countertrade units in or near their export-finance departments.

Some commercial banks also have branches in Vienna that do some countertrade work, especially East–West deals. Only one British bank has such a branch so far.

To sum up, most European commercial banks know they are not general trading companies and do not want to be. A few invest in such companies as largely passive shareholders and pass their customers' business to them. Most either try to avoid countertrade business or treat it as an aspect of financial engineering and differentiate their role from that of a trader. This third approach seems to me both valid and practical.

THE ROLE OF NONBANKS IN EUROPE

In Europe, as in the United States, the banks (both merchant and commercial) play a less dominant role in most countertrade, at least in the nonproject-related deals, than do nonfinancial companies. The big European companies like Airbus Industries, Imperial Chemical, British American Tobacco (BAT), Davy, Dassault, Thyssen, and Metalgesellschaft have their own countertrade departments or trading subsidiaries. Then there are innumerable small trading companies, not only in Vienna but in most European financial centers, many of whom profess a capability to move countertraded goods.

Countertrade Information Services

A fairly recent arrival on the company scene are the countertrade information services. These institutions are exemplified by Batis Ltd. in London and ACECO in France. These companies provide a data base on countertrade products and countertrade regulations in various countries, which subscribers may tap. They are beginning also to provide computerized matchmaking services between companies in debit to some country's counterpurchase system and those in credit or those willing to buy counterpurchase items. Batis is said to have about sixty members and ACECO, helped by official promotion, has about two hundred.

Joint Ventures in Countertrade

Some European trading companies have responded to the expansion of barter by forming international links. The best known example is MG Services, which has linked with, on the one hand, First Boston to explore the countertrade-project finance link and with, on the other hand, Dreyfus in Paris to extend each partner's geographical expertise and to complement hard-commodity experience with soft commodities. Other companies already are international—for example, those that form part of the commercial empires owned by ex-East African Asians and other groups thrown out by colonial population movement. In Italy, most countertrade is handled by trading companies partially owned by the big, public-sector corporations. IRI, the industrial combine, has a company that now operates a joint venture with Sears World Trade, for example. In Germany, associations' membership in chambers of commerce is compulsory—a factor that has long been considered positive for Germany's successful export orientation. Chambers of commerce are now playing some part in helping German companies deal with countertrade, too, by providing information and matchmaking opportunities. The German Wholesale and Foreign Trade Association also keeps information that is helpful to people trying to market countertrade goods.

Multinational Corporations

The countertrade units of the European multinational (or even some large national) corporations generally use trading companies for marketing. Exceptions to this occur when the countertrade items are products with which the company is familiar. Thus Thyssen's trading subsidiary will take countertrade goods on its own account when they are steel or metal manufactures such as Thyssen has long made and sold itself. Buy-back items from foreign projects can sometimes be handled directly by a promoter of the project (e.g., tractors by a tractor company).

Plant contractors and engineers, however, are not usually in that position. Sometimes they can draw on knowledge derived from procurement operations they carry out in managing plant construction to find buyers for buy-back or counterpurchase goods. More often they resort to appropriately specialized trading companies. Airplane manufacturers, who have done some of the largest countertrade deals, generally have the leverage to get primary commodities like oil in countertrade for their planes; the companies' internal units will evaluate and price such deals, use commodity traders to market the goods, and use banks to provide documentation and escrow arrangements.

EUROPEAN OFFICIAL ATTITUDES AND PRACTICES

Official Attitudes

Officially, the countries of Northern Europe wish to discourage countertrade— at least outside the field of offset arrangements for military sales. Official treatment of export credit has had the practical effect of promoting the specific form of counterpurchase in countertrade: official insurance is only available in countertrade deals if the obligation to repay the credit insured is independent of any other commitment the exporter may make as part of the deal. Thus the party imposing countertrade requirements must commit himself to repay his export credit and pin the exporter down to his countertrade obligations via some independent contract. Most countries will also not let aid funds be associated with countertrade obligations. In addition, governments are wary of the dumping potential in buy-back deals and the problem of countertrade deals running afoul of quantitative trade restrictions like the Multi-Fiber Agreement.

Official Practices

Despite official attitudes, most governments are in practice sympathetic and helpful to their exporters who are faced with countertrade requirements. The British Department of Trade and Industry (DTI) has issued ''Some Guidance for Exporters'' on countertrade (ten thousand copies have been distributed), and individual commercial officers in embassies can be helpful. In Sweden, the export promotion agency SUKAB is said to be helpful, and ideologically, Sweden is more apt than some European countries to support buy-back and offset deals that seem to make economic sense for the importing country. The German system of export promotion is essentially a private-sector one, but undoubtedly officials get involved in the larger and more important deals.

The French government, usually more interventionist than Britain and Germany, took the initiative to set up an agency to help French companies faced with countertrade requirements. This agency, SODICOMEX, was started a year ago with 65 percent of its capital subscribed by nine, mostly nationalized, French banks. It will not trade on its own account but acts, like most banks, as a deal structurer. Its official status gives it considerable scope in identifying potential purchasers in France and can help in dealing with foreign governments. French contractors and aircraft manufacturers have negotiated some sizable countertrade deals. One of the most famous and longest-operating countertraders with the Eastern Bloc, who has almost official status, is the French "red millionaire," Jean Baptiste Doumeng, to whom Armand Hammer is perhaps the nearest equivalent in the United States.

Italy has a structural trade deficit with the Eastern Bloc owing to its large gas imports; hence it is not under pressure such as others are to make special purchases from the Soviet Bloc. A similar position vis-à-vis Algeria has led to Italian pressure to be granted contracts in that country. As mentioned above, promotion or facilitation of countertrade more generally is carried out by trading company vehicles that are partially owned by Italian state enterprises.

Greece and Portugal, even more than Italy, are promoters of countertrade as much or more than responders to others' demands for it. To secure a Greek public-sector contract it is now, in practice, necessary at least to offer a partial offset in the form of a joint-venture operation in Greece. In addition, those who import from Greece are more likely to get contracts. The Soviet Bloc countries, as a result, have been doing well from Greek contracts since Greece runs a trade surplus with the bloc. Portugal operates a similarly ad hoc system of linking contracts to other activities of benefit to its development, particularly investments in employment and export-creating ventures.

CONCLUSION

It would be satisfying to be able to round off this brief survey with some quantitative statements on the scope of countertrade in Europe. You will not be surprised to learn that this is no more possible than it is in other regions or for the world as a whole. Clearly, the proportion of trade involved in countertrade is likely to be correlated with a country's exports to the Soviet Bloc. Germany and Finland are likely to be the most affected in Europe, whereas Italy, a large net importer from the Eastern Bloc, would be the least affected.

Sweden, which trades extensively with the Third World, is likely to have a growing involvement in countertrade. Curiously, the United Kingdom, which still has a relatively large share of its trade with the Third World, too, does not seem to be very heavily into countertrade. The official estimate is that at most 5 percent of United Kingdom trade (i.e., £ 3 billion) represents countertrade, admittedly not insignificant in absolute terms. It is probably fair to say that countertrade requirements still deter British exporters, by and large, and most medium-sized companies have avoided them. The largest companies often cannot avoid demands for barter but have nevertheless not won many orders with countertrade elements.

Metallgesellschaft's own figures seem to indicate a rising level of European consciousness of and interest in countertrade. (It has done $700 million to $800 million turnover annually, worldwide, and deals with twelve countries in the eighteen months since they started MG Services.) At the back of the British DTI booklet on countertrade, thirty-seven companies operating in Britain list themselves as "experienced in countertrade." Of them, nine are banks or banks' subsidiaries or associates. ACECO in France has some two hundred subscribers.

Nevertheless, Europe, excluding Eastern Europe, is not in the forefront of the game except in the aerospace and military areas. With the most recently publicized megadeals by Brazil, Nigeria, and the USSR, Europe appears to be falling further behind. It seems likely that we shall have to try harder, on the reasonable assumption that the foreign-exchange constraint on the Third World is going to remain tight for many years to come.

5

Countertrade with China

BERNARD E. CONOR

Trade with Eastern Europe is different from any other kind of international trade. The shortage of basic materials, which results essentially from the centrally planned nature of the system, is only one of the unique characteristics with which we must deal.

I use a broad interpretation of the word *countertrade* to mean any situation in which we have to buy something to sell something. Also, countertrade, to me, is not a business in itself. It is nothing but a market-penetration tool. If we must buy something to penetrate the market, then we will do so. However, if we can sell without buying something in exchange, we prefer to do that.

We try to avoid the traditional types of countertrade, such as straight barter of unrelated products (e.g., a ton of wheat for a load of steel). If we do get involved in one or more of the traditional types, we simply lay it off on a countertrade company; we ourselves do not get directly involved in the disposition of unwanted products from straight barter deals. For example, we sold tobacco machinery to Poland and received tobacco in exchange. Similarly, in Bulgaria we once exchanged some of our production technology for machinery. In each case we had no direct use for the product received in barter; the Polish tobacco and Bulgarian machinery were sold through a third party—a specialized countertrade company. Note that in the second example an intangible, technology, was traded: East–West countertrade is not limited to merchandise.

However, we are actively involved in offset contracts with Eastern Europe. For example, some of our manufacturing companies in Western Europe make only part of an item—the other half of which is made in Eastern Europe. The affiliates exchange the two components, and thus we have complete production in both Western and Eastern Europe. We are therefore able to penetrate the Eastern European market. We also are able to produce in Western Europe at a low cost for use in the rest of the world.

A very important point in this example is that nobody knows how to make the whole product except us. Thus we control production and distribution. Failing to maintain control has caused a serious problem for a lot of companies. We have been careful to protect ourselves against that.

Sometimes the demand by a government that we buy in order to be able to sell involves two completely separate transactions. Our clients may be unaware that they are part of a barter deal. For example, several years ago in Mexico during one of its recurring foreign-exchange crises, the border was closed for all practical purposes—including imports. AMF has some important manufacturing plants in Mexico. When they devalued the peso so severely, our products in Mexico suddenly became very economical in the world market. We started exporting so that we could get permission to import other merchandise that was needed to keep our factories running in order to supply the local market. Again, it was a very simple problem—we needed to buy something in order to sell something. Without exporting the Mexican-produced goods, we could not have gotten the raw materials to keep the factory running.

In Japan, where we have had some of our major international operations, although there was no specific restriction, it was very prudent to buy a lot of items and manufacture a lot of things in Japan in order to be able to sell there. Many customers were more receptive as a result. We have the same situation now with the filtration plants there. We find that Suntory is much more eager to buy our filters for producing their beverages if we have at least some filter-manufacturing operation in the country.

All of the rest of my comments concentrate on East–West trade, especially China—probably the world's most exciting market. In the past twenty-six years I have had the pleasure of working in many countries. I have opened up Australia, Mexico, Scandinavia, and Japan for AMF. About six years ago I became fascinated with China and thought we ought to really do something. It was the last great market possibility left on earth. We did our homework and the results have been far better than we had ever believed: China became AMF's fifth largest export market in the world, having recently passed West Germany. How did we go about it? As Jerome Levy says in chapter 16, buyers tend to get more attention than sellers: the company that wants to sell must compete against many other sellers whereas the company that comes to buy is immediately welcome. Our penetration of China was based first on building a plant in Shanghai to export. We did not really care what the product was—we had a whole series of possible products: filters, athletic equipment, electrical components, and so on. We simply wanted to get into China to learn how to do business with the Chinese. We knew that we had a lot to learn. We had learned this from our experience in other countries. One does not get smart very quickly if one does not get in there and become deeply involved. We now have three factories in China, a fourth one signed, and things are going very well. They are all ten-year deals. We refused to make a deal with the Chinese for less than 10 years. They are very happy with that, by the way, because we were saying "this is a long-term project." Our deals have taken many forms—coproduction, joint ventures, technical transfers—all of which are recognized in various ways by the Chinese government.

Our exports to China are currently about five times the volume of our imports from China. So although we have factories there that we used to penetrate the market, our exports to China are very substantial. The exports that we take from China do not necessarily come to the United States. They were created for an entirely different reason. In fact, the main purpose of all of our manufacturing in China was to penetrate parts of the world market, which we could not penetrate by other means.

AMF now has an inflated-ball plant—the first plant we put in China. We also built a plant for manufacturing small printed-circuit-board relays. We have since negotiated a seismic plant with China National Oil and Gas and, most recently, a tobacco-machinery operation with the Chinese tobacco monopoly. China is the world's largest cigarette-producing country on earth with 144 cigarette plants. We are a major supplier of tobacco-processing machinery throughout the world to most of the tobacco monopolies around the world and in the United States as well.

Each one of these deals was done for a completely different reason. The ball plant was to get us access to the world market since 90 percent of all of the inflated balls were made in Pakistan, Japan, India, and elsewhere in Asia. Many of the balls are going to Europe, which is a major importer of all of those items. The relay plant was mainly established to compete with the Japanese in world markets: the seismic plant will be primarily used to supply the Chinese market since they are importing those items from Europe and this will save them millions of dollars in hard currency. After about two years, we anticipate that they will manufacture sufficient quantities so that we will be able to take part of the production.

I would like to make one point here. I am not aware of a single successful continuing operation in China that does not involve exporting merchandise from China. It is terribly important, if you are going to do anything there, that you offer to buy something.

After nearly six years, we have learned a few things about China, but we still have a great deal to learn. Its policies are changing, but fortunately it is going in a very positive direction so we are not particularly concerned. The Japanese have finally perceived that doing business *in* China, and not just *selling to* China, is for real; they are going to start doing joint ventures and coproductions in China. Until now the Japanese have been only sellers to China, although they have licensed certain things. The Americans, the Germans, the Italians, and the French are moving very aggressively: the Japanese do not want to be left in the wings. We have to work even harder at this time.

Other authors in this book stress that for success in countertrade, probably the most important thing that is needed is imagination. You may even have to be ingenious. The efforts must begin at home: you have to determine ways to sell your top management on some novel ideas. Fortunately, that has been relatively easy for me at AMF. In my twenty-six years with the company, we have had the support of our chairmen in penetrating new markets and using countertrade. Without that senior-level support, we could have done nothing.

It may be of interest to you to hear of the development of our first venture into China. It was not a typical arrangement: we started by reading Chairman Mao's little red book. Later, while listening to our Chinese hosts, it became very clear—this was early in China's post-Mao era when it had just decided to deal with the West—that they had a number of Mao's precepts that had not left their minds as yet: never incur debt and do everything yourself. When I came back to the United States, I drafted a contract, which was presented to AMF's Advisory Council, of a revolutionary proposal for entering the China market.

We kept clearly in mind what we had heard in China and read in the "little red book" of Chairman Mao's quotations. We were convinced that the Chinese were going to change eventually, but they had not changed in 1979. We offered them a contract with some of the most unusual things you have ever seen in it. China needed about $1 million worth of machinery. The contract was drawn up to say that "this machinery is free. It belongs to AMF. It will remain ours for ten years. However, it is free for you to use." What caused me to suggest this was what I had read in the little red book and had heard about the problems of negotiating for years on a deal.

After presenting the draft document to the Chinese, I came back the next morning, and they had translated it into Chinese. In at least six paragraphs, the contract said that the machinery is free. Suddenly negotiations were very cordial and very friendly. The only question that came up was what would happen to the machinery at the end of ten years. They said, "Can we buy it?" I said, "Sure." They said, "What price?" I said, "A price to be negotiated." It is written into the contract that way.

The *Peoples' Daily*, which is the Communist party paper, described that as a countertrade agreement; they consider that they leased the machinery. It all has worked out well. It solved all of their problems, and we got the plant going. In two weeks we negotiated the deal, and by the end of the year, the plant was running. It has been running now for several years, and we have been very happy with it.

We insured the investment with the Overseas Private Investment Corporation (OPIC). Unfortunately, the treaty between the U.S. government and China had not been signed at the time. We had actually shipped the machinery before the treaty was ever signed; therefore, we could not get the OPIC insurance until about six months after the machinery was installed. Now in all of our plants in China, the machinery is insured with OPIC in Washington, so that we have the protection of the U.S. government if something goes wrong.

The next important thing to stress is patience. Another key consideration is that we insist in all of our contracts that we be permitted to have, because of quality control, one of our people in the plant at all times. We have people in Hong Kong whom we rotate into China. We control the quality. We control the flow of the machinery. We control adding new products, modifying products, correcting problems, changing labels, and whatever else has to be done. They have accepted that, and it has worked very well.

Another thing deals with the risk of licensing. All of our contracts require that we are the sole exporter of any product made on our machinery or with our know-how. We have the sole right to export it. The only time that the Chinese can export it is if we grant them specifically in writing the opportunity to ship it out themselves. The Chinese have been agreeable to such a situation. It takes a little discussion, but it is very important to protect yourself, because these plants are intended to serve the world. We ship from China in order to help us do other things there. As long as they know we are good buyers and that we can serve the rest of the world on a highly competitive basis, our imports flow very well.

There is not always a direct connection between our exports and our imports. The biggest problem that we have had in China has been with the U.S. government. The problem is export controls on sophisticated machinery, testing equipment, and so on. We have millions of dollars held up at the current time in orders that we could ship from the United States to China were it not for the U.S. government's export-control policy. Therefore, plan upon delays from this end. Leave yourself at least three to nine months.

The controls are especially restrictive in the area of computer-controlled test equipment. In all of these plants we insist upon sophisticated test equipment. We have a representative in Washington who works on these issues full time. Generally, we have had good luck, but some of them take a long time to get through.

Also, COCOM (the Coordinating Group Consultative Committee), the intergovernmental group that seeks to coordinate controls on the shipment of sophisticated equipment to Communist countries, can obstruct shipments even though we get the full approval of the Defense Department and the Commerce Department. COCOM has probably been our number one problem to date in the China operations.

In an article from the *People's Daily*, our operations in China were highlighted. It is interesting to note what was important to the Chinese. They pointed out a few key reasons: (1) They criticized themselves saying that they had a bad product; (2) they got *free* machinery and technology from AMF; (3) they got a passport to the world market. The latter is probably the greatest thing that you can take to China. They can do a lot of things, but the one thing they cannot do is to sell around the world, and that's the greatest thing that an American company can offer. They said that in 1981, the first year of operations, they made a profit of $60,000. By 1984, they indicated that the plant made a profit of $1,250,000.

When you deal with China, do not be afraid to mention profits to them. Every time I am negotiating a contract with the Chinese, I insist that they include a 20 or 25 percent profit after we get all of their costs sorted out. I said, "We won't deal with you unless you make money because you are going to be a bad supplier or a bad partner if you do not make money; you've got to make a profit." They have now come around in the past six years to the realization that profits are appealing. *Profit* is now a very acceptable word.

In addition to the ball-making, seismic, and electrical-component equipment already mentioned, some of our other activities in China may interest you. We have just opened our fourth bowling center in Beijing; China has now asked us to supply some bowling instructors so that they can train for the Olympics; they are hoping that in Korea bowling will be offered as an Olympics sport. We also export baking machinery. We sold the Elee Bakery a machine that makes four hundred hamburger buns a minute. They wanted one that made six hundred, but our people convinced them that it was too big. Tire-retreading equipment, stitching equipment, and gymnastics and sports equipment are further exports. A year ago they asked us if we would be their buying agent for all of the equipment to equip the Chinese Olympic Teams—including the things that we did not make. We purchased things such as diving boards, archery equipment, and sailboats from nine other American companies for which we were paid a satisfactory fee. We are now working with them in oil-field services and on a whole series of other products. Our willingness to buy something first has helped us to sell something. Because we are doing all of these other things and they know that we are a good partner, money has not been a problem. The Bank of China has no trouble opening letters of credit. For things they want, they will pay you cash. Do not worry about it. It is not a problem if you handle it right.

Things have changed quickly in China. Six years ago when I went there, we would go into a room to negotiate. On the wall behind the Chinese were pictures of Mao, Lenin, and Stalin. A year later there were pictures of Mao and Lenin. The third year there was only Lenin. The fourth year there was a picture of the caves from where Mao and Chou En Lai had the long march. Last year in the same place, in two of the original picture frames, were two pictures of AMF bowling centers!

PART III

COUNTERTRADE PRACTICES IN DIFFERENT INDUSTRIAL SECTORS

6

Countertrade in a Project-Development Company

JACQUES ROSTAIN

The field of countertrade is very dynamic, not only in the types of activities involved but even in its terminology.

DEFINITIONS

Countertrade

Countertrade is a general term covering all forms of trade whereby a seller (e.g., an exporter) or an assignee is required to accept goods or services from the buyer (e.g., the importer or the importing country) as either full or partial payment. It is an "umbrella" term covering a variety of commercial arrangements including classical barter, compensation, buy-back, and counterpurchase or offset.

Barter

Classical (i.e., pure or simple) *barter* involves the direct exchange of goods at an agreed rate between two parties. There is no exchange of money, and usually, there are two parties involved in a one-shot transaction. For example, Argentina once exchanged corn for Cuban sugar. The Argentine Central Bank kept the books and debited the trade when a ton of corn was exported and credited it when a ton of sugar reached Buenos Aires. As another example of classical barter, in 1977 Brazil exchanged 50,000 tons of Brazilian soybeans for 50,000 tons of Mexican black beans.

Compensation Agreements

Compensation agreements involve an arrangement whereby an exporter will accept a specified amount of products from the importer as a full or partial payment in kind. Full compensation deals are similar to classical barter. However, a currency of exchange is used, and each party bills for his own shipment. Furthermore, the exporter can assign his commitment to a third party. Partial compensation deals involve partial currency payment, and the rest is in local products. For example, Iran has paid for many of its imports partially in cash and partially in barrels of crude oil.

Buy-Back

The form of countertrade known as *buy-back* is often considered a variation of compensation. It is a type of agreement involving an exporter of machinery, equipment, technology, or two or three of these things, who agrees to receive payment in products manufactured by the equipment exported or technology sold. An example is the sale of the pipeline to the USSR, which is being paid for in natural gas. Another example would be the sale of a textile factory for which the buyer pays with textiles produced in that factory.

Counterpurchase or Offset

Counterpurchase or *offset* involves two contracts. The first is for the sale of goods with the exporter receiving full payment in convertible currency upon delivery (or, if credit is extended, over a period). The second contract requires the exporter to purchase a specific amount of products from the importing country over a certain period. For example, Indonesia requires a counterpurchase for every sale of more than $500,000. The exporter gets paid for its sale but must agree to purchase the equivalent of the value of the sales contract within a specified period. For noncompliance, there is a penalty of 50 percent of the value of the sale.

Offset is usually used by developing countries in their military hardware purchases. Some industrialized countries also employ it. For example, Canada has an offset program for its purchase of planes for the Canadian Air Force with the primary emphasis upon the transfer of technology for use by Canada.

Switch

A *switch trade* is a triangular transaction paid for in clearing dollars for goods moving to a third country.

THE VOLUME OF COUNTERTRADE

An unpublished report by the General Agreement on Tariff and Trade (GATT) in 1984 said that barter accounts for about 8 percent of world merchandise trade. However, this figure is overly conservative, and we should think in terms of 10 to 20 percent as more realistic. There is no doubt that countertrade, as a requirement, has spread among many countries. For example in Europe the list of countries includes the Eastern Bloc, Yugoslavia, Greece, Turkey, and, for certain defense offsets, all of the developed countries. In Asia, countries actively using countertrade include Australia, Indonesia, Malaysia, and the People's Republic of China. In South America, we can mention Mexico, Brazil, Ecuador, Argentina, and Peru. In Africa, Algeria, Tunisia, and Egypt can all be mentioned.

As each country has developed its own set of rules and regulations, every countertrade deal has to be tailor-made. There are no laws, ground rules, standard procedures, or standard contracts. What is acceptable in one case may not be in a repeat performance the following day. Every deal is time consuming, difficult to conclude, and full of pitfalls. However, when a deal is done satisfactorily, we have achieved our purpose—that is, selling our products or services.

ORGANIZING FOR COUNTERTRADE AT COMBUSTION ENGINEERING

Combustion Engineering is composed of about thirty-five companies, all of which are involved in export markets. The company derives possibly 40 percent of its income from international trade.

At the end of the 1970s, Combustion Engineering (CE) thought that barter and countertrade would become an increasingly necessary component of the financing of international projects. As a result, CE established CE Trading in 1980. The responsibility of CE Trading is to arrange and accept all countertrade obligations associated with the sales of the company's products and services. Since 1981 CE Trading and our international project-finance group have worked closely together to develop the financial architecture of projects involving our commercial proposals.

CE Trading has built up a professional staff, supported by an interactive relationship network with the world's major trading companies and banks. Our company is capable of making or arranging a market for a wide range of countertrade or buy-back products. We work with an intimate knowledge of CE's own internal needs for raw materials, commodities, and finished or semifinished goods (CE purchases in excess of $2 billion annually), as well as the needs of our clients and major trading companies. CE Trading had completed and executed approximately $300 million in countertrade obligations by 1984. Working with the many CE companies, CE Trading is pursuing projects to be awarded within the next two years, which have a countertrade requirement in excess of an additional $500 million.

Since the fall of 1984, CE Trading has also undertaken to develop business for third parties. Our norm is to accept clients in fields that are noncompetitive with our own and in areas where we have had some experience and where our expertise will help to conclude countertrade transactions. We intend to have about ten to twenty such clients and work actively on their behalf.

We have approached the problem in a conservative way, and we maintain a small staff in the United States, as well as contacts with some of our key financial people throughout Europe and agents in countries where none of our companies have their own offices. This gives us a certain flexibility and, at the same time, keeps our overhead low and manageable.

We are not interested in developing our own sales network for our countertrade commitments, nor are we planning to hire traders in oil, shoes, or metals—to mention a few areas where countertrade goes on. We will find the group or company whom we consider best suited for the particular deal and ask them to work with us on a case-by-case basis.

PITFALLS TO AVOID

We always keep in mind that in any countertrade there is a third partner, the host government or one of its agencies. Without its blessing, nothing can be done. The government is the most important player and a good understanding of its requirements and aims is vital. This is where our people on the spot perform an invaluable role.

To give you a specific example, in the Eastern Bloc countries, the foreign-trade organization (FTO) that is interested in buying from us will try to arrange both sides of the deal. However, this greatly limits our flexibility in choosing the products to accept in exchange. Our interest is to have the maximum amount of flexibility via the freedom to purchase from other FTOs in that country while getting the credit against our sale. In Yugoslavia, matters are complicated by the fact that one republic does not readily deal with another; for example, the issue of interrepublic exchange of foreign currencies can be introduced only at the highest level. Therefore, in that country, patience is a necessary virtue. In one specific case, we had to wait two years to get a license. It was finally granted, but by then the market conditions had changed, and the sale was no longer possible.

Regarding legal technicalities, it is always better to have two contracts (i.e., counterpurchase)—one for the sale and one for the purchase. Furthermore, ideally, the purchase contract should be assignable to a third party; when such an assignment can occur (with the full acknowledgment of the authorities), our countertrade risks can be eliminated.

We also prefer an agreement covering the broadest list of goods with no restrictions on the destinations and with a clear understanding that they will be offered at competitive world prices. If the agreement requires additionality, we shall spell out what it means and will include the concept of substitution. (If we do not increase the volume of exports, we can sometimes argue that we are displacing sales from other origins). The time frame is also important: the more flexibility we may have, the less pressure we will be under to sell on unfavorable terms.

PENALTY CLAUSES

We always try to include a penalty clause that is fair to both parties. We think that a range of 5 to 10 percent is reasonable. But no matter what penalty is included in the contract, we make all efforts to comply with the countertrade requirements, sometimes regardless of the cost. If we do not execute the countertrade, we may be black-listed; that could lead to very serious problems for some of our units.

FORCE MAJEURE

All countertrade contracts should make allowance for unintended and uncontrollable interruptions. Strikes, countervailing duties, embargoes, and nondelivery of products can and do happen. Some of these risks can be insured. We believe that such insurance costs are reasonable and can be included in our sales price; insurance should be used to the maximum extent.

If commodities are involved, we always try to hedge them. We are not speculators: we try to be deal makers.

SIZE OF TRANSACTION

Our transactions range from $500,000 to $100 million. For practical purposes, we prefer $10 million to $20 million contracts; there is as much time and energy spent on such a deal as is spent on a transaction of $100,000. Larger contracts can become burdensome obligations.

We try to keep up with all of the information regarding countertrade. There are times when regulations change in the middle of a transaction. Furthermore, we need to know the efforts of the competition. In some of our offers (e.g., in engineering or power projects), the buying country requires six months or longer to evaluate our proposal. Upon acceptance, we need to be ready to proceed on short notice to negotiate a final contract for the countertrade. Therefore, in order that no time is lost on our part, we need to be fully aware of all current conditions that might affect the attractiveness of the contract to us.

THE ATTITUDE OF THE U.S. GOVERNMENT

The American government has an ambivalent attitude toward countertrade. On the one hand, officials of the Department of Commerce have gone every year to mainland China and advised Chinese officials on countertrade and its practice. Furthermore, in 1983 the U.S. Department of Agriculture bartered with Jamaica substantial amounts of U.S. powdered milk for Jamaican bauxite. Yet one wonders whether an official position in favor of countertrade will ever be stated by U.S. officials.

Indeed, the general position of the government is critical of countertrade. Below is an outline of the seven policy guidelines that sources say represents current White House policy on countertrade:

1. The U.S. government generally views countertrade as contrary to an open, free trading system.

2. The U.S. government opposes *government-mandated* countertrade and will raise these concerns with the relevant governments.

3. However, as a matter of policy, the U.S. government will not oppose U.S. companies' participation in countertrade arrangements unless such action could have a negative impact on national security.

4. The U.S. government will provide advisory and market intelligence services to U.S. businesses, including information on the application of U.S. trade laws to countertrade goods.

5. The U.S. government will continue to review financing for projects containing countertrade/barter on a case-by-case basis, taking account of the distortions caused by them.

6. The U.S. government will participate in reviews of countertrade in the International Monetary Fund (IMF), the Organization for Economic Cooperation and Development (OECD), and the GATT.

7. The U.S. government will exercise caution in the use of its barter authority, reserving it for these situations that offer advantages not offered by conventional market operations.

Also, the International Monetary Fund has always been against countertrade since it believes the practice does restrict free trade.

THE BASIS FOR SUCCESSFUL COUNTERTRADE

In summary, here is a list of the criteria that we at CE believe are critical for success in countertrade operations:

1. We prefer to handle products that are noncompetitive and complementary with our own—and of equivalent quality. Indeed, a diversity of products using our existing market capabilities may actually help to cushion against market downturn.

2. It is important that we can leverage the capabilities of our existing sales organization. By keeping our staff small and using wherever possible our own sales force, we limit expenses.

3. Our trading activity needs to be consistent with both corporate goals and field-operation activities.

4. The establishment of clearly defined objectives is very important. Often the counter-trade product may not contribute a profit, but the added sales to the company will.

5. In order for us to use the company's buying power to satisfy our barter obligations, the countertrade department must educate our buyers to use foreign sources of products for CE's needs. This is one of the most difficult areas. It requires patience to obtain the results needed. Our approach has been to start slowly and continue to move slowly.

In conclusion, we at CE view countertrade in today's world market as a necessary evil. To compete, we must be prepared to meet all of the barter requirements so that we may win the order. We must keep abreast of all changing regulations, be prepared to travel to all corners of the world, and try to find imaginative solutions to an ever-growing problem so that our sales can expand.

7

The International Offset Phenomenon in the Aerospace Industry

L. DUKE GOLDEN

If we do not learn to understand and guide the great forces of change at work on our world today, we may find ourselves swallowed up by vast upheavals in our way of life. Countertrade is one of those upheavals. In my twenty-five years in international business, I have never seen a phenomenon with the magnitude of change that countertrade has caused.

OFFSET

Offset is the principal form of countertrade in the aerospace industry. *Offset* is a type of counterpurchase whereby a supplier assists its foreign buyer in reducing the latter's trade imbalance caused by the purchase of the supplier's products. The country to which the obligation is owed is called the "commitment country." For example, U.S Aerospace Corporation (USAC) might offer to "offset" part of the cost of its sales to a foreign purchaser of USAC aircraft. If USAC sells $700 million to $800 million of airplanes to country X, that country has a significant trade imbalance caused by the sale. It is not unlikely that the country will ask USAC to assist it during a period of time in dealing with that imbalance by assisting the export of some of its goods and services.

The aerospace and defense-products industries deal with long-term offsets. Most offset contracts are for ten to twelve years. Thus, offset is not something that has to be done on a one-transaction basis.

A special form of offset is called "liquidity trade." Liquidity trade occurs when the dollar amount and the payment period of the countertrade of products or services *from* the commitment country are equivalent to the amount and period of the product sold *to* the commitment country. The proceeds from the liquidity trade will be used by the commitment country to pay for the imports whose purchase had caused the country to impose the commitment obligation. Countertrades may either be done by the company that incurred the obligation or by a third party on behalf of that company.

It is very important to USAC that it can help its customer generate the necessary hard currency with which to get paid. Some liquidity trades may be as short as six months whereas some may be much longer.

DIRECT OFFSET VERSUS INDIRECT OFFSET

There are two basic forms of offset: direct and indirect.

Direct offset involves coproduction in a foreign country by both USAC and the buying country of part of a USAC product that the country is buying. Thus the offset relates directly to USAC's sale to that country. This obviously provides a variety of local benefits to the buying country. The agreement may or may not involve a buy-back arrangement requiring USAC to buy part of that joint production.

Coproduction agreements usually require technical assistance. If the coproduction agreement involves technology transfer, permission by the U.S government is sometimes required.

Indirect offset refers to an offset commitment by USAC to arrange for the purchase of goods or services that are not directly related to the goods that USAC sold. The purchases of such products may be made by USAC or by other buyers with USAC acting as a "facilitator" of the international transactions. Normally, the actual trade is concluded through trading companies.

In liquidity trades the hard currency that is generated is placed in an escrow account. Then letters of credit that are issued to USAC are drawn against that escrow account to effect payment to USAC.

Major indirect countertrade transactions by USAC are called "project trades." This involves USAC's assistance on a specific project in the commitment country: for example, the swapping of Spanish clinker cement (which is the cooked limestone before it is ground up and the additives put into it to make finished cement) to the U.S. in exchange for coal that will be used by the Spanish cement companies. USAC could arrange the complete package including the shipping. When the transaction is completed, USAC would earn $20 million to $25 million of offset. When the project system is completed, USAC will have little to do. Once the "pump" is structured and operating the project will continue to generate offset.

A project in Spain completed by the Northrop Corporation involved an $11 million repair of a vessel in a Spanish shipyard. Unemployment is a very serious problem in Spain. This project will give many workers full employment. This is a good example of offset that not only helps fulfill an offset obligation but also makes a very positive contribution to the economy of the commitment country.

THE SIZE AND ORIGIN OF INTERNATIONAL OFFSET

Nobody really knows how big offset is. The study that Willis Bussard discusses in chapter 2 shows that between 1980 and 1981 for the companies surveyed, there was a 50 percent increase in countertrade. From 1981 to 1982 there was a 64 percent increase, and from 1982 to 1983 there was a 117 percent increase.

Also, a survey that was described in a paper at the International Countertrade Conference in Vienna last year indicated that by 1988 about 40 percent of all international trade will be countertrade and by the turn of the century it may be 50 percent. The defense products industry believes that about 65 percent (by dollar value) of its total international business involves offset in some form.

Modern international countertrade began with the Eastern Bloc countries after World War I. However, it soon spread to developing countries. My first countertrade transaction was in the 1960s when I was with the Kaiser Jeep organization. We had assembly plants around the world that assembled Jeep vehicles from the knocked-down components that we shipped to them. In one transaction, Colombia came to Kaiser to buy Jeeps for the military, but they only had coffee with which to pay. To implement the sale, we accepted the coffee, exchanged it to West Germany for machinery, swapped the machinery from West Germany to Israel. Then Israel paid dollars to our Toledo operation for completely knocked-down Jeeps that were shipped to Israel, assembled, and reshipped over to Colombia. The transaction took about a year to put together, but it showed a trend of what would come in the future.

Later, while still at Kaiser, we arranged a reciprocal trade with Japan. We purchased $110 million of ships in exchange for a Japanese commitment to ship $110 million of cargoes on our ships. That trade was the beginning of the Kaiser Shipping Corporation. The Japanese had never before had anyone actually ask them to do a reciprocal trade. Although it took three years, we got that trade.

SPECIAL ISSUES IN OFFSET

Incremental Trade

Indirect offset efforts often involve working with other companies that purchase goods and services acceptable to the commitment country. If the transactions involve incremental costs, USAC will call them "incremental trades."

Such incremental trading is used by some aerospace companies to fulfill their offset requirements. For example, a USAC may call a trading company and say, "If you will do certain business from Country X, we will pay you a commission and perhaps cover any incremental cost."

Incremental trading is extremely important in liquidity trades. When USACs do not act as trading companies, to move great quantities of products in a short period to generate hard currency, they must use a trading company or companies.

Third-Party Technology Transfers

There are times when a USAC is able to find technology that a commitment country needs. Such technology is either to produce a new product for export or improve an existing exported product. Many times technical assistance is also provided with the technology.

Counterinvestment

Another offset technique that USACs sometimes use is the assistance of a company that is interested in making an investment in the commitment country. The USAC normally only facilitates the financing and does not make direct investments. For example, a USAC may find the working capital to finance a better marketing group for a product that will be imported from the commitment country into the United States.

Counterpurchase

In counterpurchase, USAC sells its products to Country X and directly buys back certain products for its own use. Some aerospace companies have set up special groups to coordinate such counterpurchases by the companies and their suppliers.

Offset requirements clearly involve the need for a company to be very flexible and creative. My favorite story about countertrade involves the man who came home from work and told his family he was being transferred to Jedda and that they would have to sell the family dog. His little boy was very disturbed. However, the next day when his father came home the son was happy to tell him that he had sold the family dog for two hundred dollars. His dad was delighted, and asked, "Son, what are you going to do with two hundred dollars?" The son said, "Well, Dad, I didn't exactly get dollars, I got two $100 cats." Similarly, in many countertrade contracts, you may feel that your real job is selling $100 cats.

Legislated Countertrade

An increasing number of countries are mandating that large import contracts must be at least partially offset by purchases from the importing country. Indonesia is perhaps best known in this area, but many Latin American countries are now moving into those ranks. There is typically a severe penalty clause for failure to comply with the agreement.

From a lawyer's perspective, the downside risk in this type of obligation is the amount of the penalty. However, as a practical matter, the amount of the penalty is not the key issue. No substantial American defense-products marketer will ever allow itself to get into a position where it would have to pay the penalty for failing to perform its offset commitment. The day a company pays that penalty, it has failed; when you fail in a country, you never do business there again. Word travels fast in this business—the loss-of-business penalty would likely be far greater than that specified in the penalty clause.

One of the big problems for some USACs in the past was the lack of involvement in the sale contract. The product would be sold by marketing people who would have no responsibility for fulfilling the offset obligation. Marketing people obviously are eager to sell their product and sometimes give inadequate thought to the difficulties of satisfying the offset obligations they accept. An agreement might be signed that merely said that USAC will export $200 million of the commitment country's products over a specified period. Then the obligations are turned over to others to perform.

Fortunately, some USACs have changed this approach. Now, those in the offset group play a significant role in the preparation and negotiation of the offset section of the sales contract. What they are trying to do is to get away from selling "$100 cats." I have nothing against cats, but the wrong cat can turn out to be a real dog!

Today some USACs consider offset as an integral part of their sales contracts. First, however, the basic sales contract must be sound and attractive to the buyer. A USAC cannot sell its products to a country if the country does not want the product. Offset will not sell to a buyer what is not needed. However, everything else being equal, if a USAC has a better offset program than its competition, offset can play a significant role in selling that USAC's products.

I believe the offset program in some situations can be as important as but not more important than the product. Offset is a political tool used by most countries to justify large military hardware purchases to their constituents. Thus government officials can tell their constituents when they have spent $700 million or $800 million for defense products, "Don't worry about it. We will get it all back, because the supplier has promised us that all of this money that we spent will be replaced by new export sales." The offset objective of most foreign governments is to improve the balance of trade, reduce unemployment, and achieve self-sufficiency.

International countertrade is a fact of international life. Offset is not going to go away. Thus USACs must be prepared to respond to customers' requests when asked. To be able to respond, the USAC should concentrate its offset efforts in an in-house offset group. This group should be given strong support at the corporate level. I suggest that such an offset department be organized into four prime functions. Offset sourcing and distribution offices should be established in countries where the USAC has significant offset commitments. The manager's job there would be to find a source for the product in that country and to provide liaison with the government. Trade operations should primarily be a project-trading type of function. Offset-product development should involve the technology-transfer concept mentioned earlier. Administration and planning should be responsible for computerizing offset information and activities and play a major role in proposal preparation.

An in-house offset group will enable the USAC to become self-sufficient in project trades and to work efficiently and knowledgeably with trading companies in spot trades.

The most important factor in countertrade is imagination. An example of imagination is second-tier liquidity trades. A company in Switzerland wants to sell its products to Mexico, but Mexico does not have the hard currency. A second-tier liquidity trade will generate the hard currency in Mexico so that the Swiss company can be paid in hard currency and sell its product. More important, the USAC earns offset credits in Switzerland.

Financing and shipping knowledge are important parts of an offset program. All of you who have been involved in trading know that in many trades there is as much money to be made in the financing and transporting of the product as there is in selling it. Also, there can be as much money lost. Excellent advice can be given to commitment countries in the ancillary services to a trade—shipping, financing, and insurance.

Today, one of the largest chores of a national company involved in big offset is liaison with the commitment country's government. This is important to make sure, before working on a particular offset transaction, that the transaction will be accredited as offset. One of the first questions that we should ask when a prospective offset transaction is contemplated is, "Do you know if it's going to count as offset?" Two key concepts here are additionality and linkage.

Additionality means that the product that you propose to export from the commitment country is something that (1) is not now being exported from that country; (2) is a surplus, traditionally exported product; or (3) is one where the buyer is a new customer. The secret of additionality is cooperation with the government of the commitment country. If that country's government wants the USAC product, its demands for additionality will be moderate. One of the advantages a USAC has in our industry is the good relationship with the government because of the priority of its products. This may enable better sourcing than some major international trading companies. The whole area of additionality is really the relationship with the local government.

The second factor is *linkage*—a clear connection or "link" between the efforts of the USAC in the particular transaction and the offset that is later claimed. To me, linkage is critically important. Some companies in the world play games in offset. They try to claim offset credits for deals with which they really had no "linkage." They contributed nothing to the deal, not even a commission. Thus some governments are becoming very nervous about "linkage." Korea has strong feelings about linkage. Australia is another country that has had bad experiences in the past with people committing to offset and then playing games.

International trade is a tough business. Offset (or countertrade, barter, liquidity trades, counterpurchase) has become a key ingredient in international trade. The most important single factor to being successful in countertrade is imagination. A second important element is detail. Numerous trades fail on details. It is amazing how many times a buyer and a seller are ready to deal but the transaction fails on the details. I believe that USACs should turn offset from a problem into an opportunity.

In the field of countertrade, if you are imaginative and are careful about details, you can be very successful. If you are careless, you may find yourself with some products that will be difficult for you to sell or other obligations that will be difficult for you to satisfy.

8

The Death and Growth of Countertrade Subsidiaries in the Consumer-Products Industry

STEPHEN E. CRAIN

When I was invited by Christopher Korth to participate in the University of South Carolina conference in 1985, I was still a member of the staff of a major computer manufacturer's trade/countertrade subsidiary. For several months my colleagues and I had been anticipating the imminent demise of our once proud group headquartered jointly in the United States and Vienna. Together with a Viennese colleague, we were able to market our services as a package to a countertrade consortium consisting of a British consumer-products manufacturer and a Swedish equipment manufacturer.

When I first joined this organization in 1980 (shortly after the Soviet invasion of Afghanistan), I discovered a talented and energetic group of individuals who had formulated and implemented a highly innovative East–West trade strategy. It has been only during the past three years that this group has tumbled from its once lofty leadership role in the world of countertrade to that of virtual non-participant. What went wrong and why?

This multinational corporation (MNC) met its first countertrade requirements some twelve years ago, born out of the early days of détente. The original transactions were for the most part not very sophisticated but mainly straight, classical barter deals. Over the years the MNC's efforts grew more and more sophisticated and innovative as it struggled to meet its ever-changing requirements.

OUTSIDE EVENTS

The outside events consist of only two items: (1) the international political climate and (2) the foreign trade organizations' "desk-to-desk" requirement that we satisfy our countertrade obligation by buying from the same ministry to which we sold our products.

There is no way that one can effectively overstate the effect of the Soviet invasion of Afghanistan and the subsequent Carter administration ban on the sale of high technology upon the entire marketing strategy of the U.S. computer industry in Eastern Europe.

The second issue that cannot be ignored is the "desk-to-desk" requirements of almost all foreign trade ministries in Eastern Europe. As Jacques Rostain mentions in chapter 6, it is highly desirable whenever possible to avoid such bilateral limitations in bartering with Eastern Europe; unfortunately, it often is not possible. Our group found it very difficult in many instances either to use in-house or to market outside of the company much of the equipment, products, or components sourced from the various ministries of electronics in Eastern Europe. For the most part, their computer industry lags our Western state-of-the-art technology by at least two (and often more) generations. The only real outlet for such technology is in Third World nations. Even there we find that they covet the latest technologies found only in the West.

DEVELOPMENTS WITHIN THE CORPORATION

The second group of influences on the demise of our trading group is somewhat more lengthy and probably a lot less well documented—as well as being very much more subjective. This list contains items such as internal politics, corporate organization, and personnel. These are tricky subjects individually and collectively. They can be volatile.

Internal Politics

When our vice-chairman, a great advocate of East–West trade, retired late in 1983, we lost our corporate "godfather." His retirement marked the beginning of the end of our countertrade effort in Eastern Europe. Without this clear line of authority directly to top management, as well as a continuation of management's clear mandate and its vision of our overall function within the corporate structure, our group had little chance of survival.

Corporate Organization

In January of 1982 in response to the then-proposed Export Trading Company Act, the small staff of the marketing-support countertrade group was organized into a separate profit center with the goal of creating a full-scale trading house. This changeover from a cost center of a marketing division to a "stand-alone" profit center was perhaps the nail in the coffin of our small countertrade group. This nail remained "unhammered" for nearly three years, but in the end it was this issue more than any other that killed us.

For the most part, countertrade alone should not be considered by a manufacturing company to be a viable means of making money. It is only a means to an end, that end supposedly being the successful consummation of a sale of a firm's products or services into the target nation. As Jacques Rostain concluded in chapter 6, countertrade is a necessary evil of doing business in nations that are short of hard currencies. Only rarely, if ever, will countertrade directly generate an operating profit as a "stand-alone" transaction—at least in companies that use countertrade as a means to stimulate their sales of future production (i.e., as opposed to companies that are attempting to dispose of existing inventories).

Personnel and Operational Procedures

When the small countertrade group was merged in 1982 into the new trading subsidiary, the countertrade staff found itself for the most part no longer directly interfacing with our corporate marketing staff but instead to the corporate domestic finance group. Our new trading subsidiary was quickly staffed with a variety of corporate insiders—many of whom had little or no international experience—and even fewer with any trade or countertrade experience.

Consider as well the necessity of effectuating a counterpurchase contract using the same bureaucratic guidelines as required by company policy to finalize a computer-system contract. The legal and accounting systems at any manufacturing company are by design strict and somewhat inflexible, rendering them almost impossible to use in any sort of trading situation. Imagine the necessity of using this unwieldy system in an environment that requires innovative risk taking, methods of alternative financing, timing issues, and so on. It is an almost impossible task.

SUMMARY

This giant MNC has ceased its countertrade operations at a time when this form of trade is becoming increasingly more prevalent. The demise of our countertrade group was seemingly unnecessary. Given the proper management mandate, an interested "godfather" to represent such an unorthodox operation to senior management, and the appropriate organizational niche within the corporate structure (i.e., affiliated with the export marketing group), it could have remained a most viable marketing instrument for the various regional and country-management teams. This MNC is now a virtual nonparticipant in transactions requiring counterpurchase or offset. What few requirements remain are handled by the country executive as well as possible. It remains an inefficient (at best) and ineffective marketing/financial tool.

What is noted above is not meant to reflect adversely upon the corporation or its management but is simply an attempted evaluation and personal theory of several current and former employees. The combination of circumstances could have happened to anyone in a similar situation. There are lessons, however, that those engaged or considering participation in the volatile world of countertrade can and should learn from our experience.

A NEW OPPORTUNITY

To effectively contrast the experience noted above, consider the example of another multinational that has recently become heavily involved with the necessity of assisting some of its partners in various nations in securing the necessary hard currency required to purchase its product lines.

Like most firms, my new employer (a British multinational) met its first counterpurchase requirements on an ad hoc "as needed" basis using its foreign franchise managers. However, this method is unwieldy and highly inefficient at best, as well as drawing away the attention of a country-franchise manager from his primary mission—which is hopefully to market its own products and services into the target nation.

Recognizing the inefficiencies inherent in such a system, this group has gradually developed an organization solely responsible for the ever-increasing countertrade requirements. This evolution has been gradual during the past several years.

As director of North American Trade operations, I am responsible for establishing a "pull" strategy of marketing products received by our franchise managers in various nations of Eastern and Central Europe, as well as the nations of the Mediterranean basin and North Africa, to meet their counterpurchase or offset requirements. Traveling frequently into these nations with my franchise colleagues, I identify and contract for products that we believe may be "marketable" into the Western Hemisphere.

We are involved in such diverse product lines as lead crystal, wines, spirits, apple-juice concentrates, canned fruits, tomato paste, orange-juice concentrate, and paper products and printing. All of these programs fit into our diverse corporate requirements in some way. Many of these products can be used internally within our manufacturing entities. Others must be marketed to outside concerns.

Unlike high-tech firms that find their product lines very high on the priority lists of the various five-year plans, our firm markets a consumer product that is generally very much lower on the list of priority imports. Add to this the small-ticket and ongoing nature of our product lines in contrast to the large-ticket, one-time nature of a computer transaction, and one begins to understand the constant urgency and excellence required of our counterpurchase efforts.

This very nature of our business makes it not only inherently more difficult to perform, but gives rise to a far different set of operational risks and problems. Many of the ground rules noted above could well be applicable to our countertrade operations as well. Fortunately, the firm's management has been able most effectively to avoid these pitfalls as they have formulated their countertrade strategies.

We have a constant struggle with the Eastern Bloc regarding the quality of products they offer. For example, I have a colleague in Vienna and another in London who spend about 50 percent of their time overseeing the quality of the products we have received. We have been offered both oxidized wines and fermented apple juice. We have grown more and more sophisticated in these things during the past couple of years. But you have to be very cautious, and you have to develop a system or use people that will allow you to monitor very carefully the quality, because that quality, especially from Eastern Europe, is not consistent, even from shipment to shipment.

CONCLUSIONS

Despite the disappointing demise of the excellent countertrade operation of my former employer and the difficulties of implementing an effective barter operation, I am very bullish on countertrade. There are tremendous opportunities. It is never boring. You are always working on something a little different each time. It is not like the typical workaday world. I am grateful for the opportunities I have had these past five years to be involved in it. It opens up tremendous new horizons, and there is excellent opportunity there.

PART IV

RECENT DEVELOPMENTS IN TECHNICAL ASPECTS OF COUNTERTRADE

9

A Bank's Role in Facilitating and Financing Countertrade

JAMES M. BARKAS

Willis Bussard indicated in chapter 2 that many companies use commercial banks to assist them in countertrade. This chapter examines some of the roles that such banks can play.

THE BANKER AS BROKER AND FINANCIER OF COUNTERTRADE TRANSACTIONS

For a bank, a countertrade capability can play the role of a catalyst in the development of new business. It provides an innovative means of serving our customers by focusing our

- Resources
- Global network
- Corporate relationships
- Financial product expertise
- Integrity

on the needs of our valued customers. Essentially, a bank achieves this goal by identifying, developing, and consummating countertrade transactions. We do this by linking exporters, who have a counterpurchase requirement, with interested buyers of those products and services offered by the importer or importing country. Once the partnership is established, banks can structure the transaction, lay off the risks, and finance the deal.

Finding the Buyers for Countertrade Obligations

Novice credit analysts learn that in banking you have to identify your source of payback for a loan *before* you make the loan. However, later as lending officers, we often make loans without looking adequately at the sources of payback; as a result, we may well end up with very risky loans on our books that will never be paid. In countertrade, the problem is similar: it is very important that the company know *before* signing a contract from where the payback will come. Only after that is known should it actually structure the contract.

A counterpurchase obligation can be of two types: either the purchase of specified merchandise or the acceptance of inconvertible currencies or clearing credits; the latter generally can be used only for subsequent purchase of local goods or services.

Corresponding to these two types of counterpurchase obligations, there are two basic groups of "intermediaries" that can assist the committed company in satisfying its obligation. The first is an entity that could buy or otherwise dispose of bartered *goods* that our customer is destined to acquire. The second would comprise those entities that could use the local inconvertible currency rather than specific merchandise.

The first group of intermediaries are those that will take the counterpurchased goods and convert them into cash. Potential buyers include trading companies, merchandisers, small specialized importers, end users, and barter brokers. The second group of intermediaries involves those that can use the inconvertible currency for the purchase of local services. These users of local currencies can obviate their need for hard-cash outlays elsewhere, or they can ultimately convert the service into something of hard-cash value later in time.

Some of the potential users of local currencies include universities, movie studios, corporate research and development programs, consulting firms, promoters of tourism, nonprofit business-development groups, advertising agencies, and charities. Movie studios, for example, have been using blocked funds of their distributors to finance and fund movies in countries like Pakistan, Mexico, Egypt, and India. The studios use local currency for many of their filming expenses; thus they are able to create an asset with hard-currency value (i.e., the movie) out of what banks call a "nonperforming" asset—the blocked currencies.

Matching the Intermediaries with the Exporters

After a bank enlists the support of a wide base of intermediaries, it identifies their priorities and capabilities in terms of products and countries. Using this intermediary base we are able to select the appropriate intermediary for our client, the exporter who needs a buyer for the products he is offered by his importing customer. In so doing, we also match the country capabilities of the intermediary, the exporter, and the bank. Among the three of us, either the intermediary, the exporter, or the bank must have the in-country capability and network to link the export sale to the counterpurchase with the approval of the host-country authorities.

As an example, we advised an importer of furniture made in Yugoslavia to commit to increasing its purchases on the proviso that the incremental purchases would secure the right to make a "retour sale" or countersale back to the foreign supplier. However, despite the desirability of the incremental exports to the exporting country, the U.S. importer was encountering some difficulties in obtaining decisions, approvals, and even responses to some of its correspondence and inquiries. We helped the furniture importer obtain the necessary local approvals due to our long-term relationships with principals in the host country. The next step involved introducing the furniture importer to a U.S. exporter who wanted to sell various products to the Yugoslavian furniture manufacturer.

Note that in this example we first found the U.S. importer who would be the counterpurchaser. Then we found the U.S. exporter who already had accepted or who was considering accepting a counterpurchase obligation.

Countersales are perhaps the best way to do East European countertrade. First you find a buyer of the product who would qualify as a counterpurchaser. Then you get the approval from the commitment country to use that product as a counterpurchase. Finally, you find a company that wants to sell to the commitment country. This particular customer was buying bookcases. It was not difficult for us to find suitable suppliers of sandpaper, lacquer, glue, and veneer, all to be used in the production of the bookcases.

This is a particularly good example of a three-way deal where all parties benefited. The importer got the furniture at a small discount because of a subsidy from the supplier of the lacquer and the sandpaper. The quality of the bookcases was improved because of the use of better materials. The U.S. supplier of the lacquer and the sandpaper found a cash-paying customer in the Balkans (with funds received from the U.S. importer). Yugoslavia itself developed a major export market and was able to expand this particular export flow into a series of related flows. The bank was financially rewarded and also strengthened its ties with two customers and the foreign government.

Expanding Partnerships—Growing to New Products/New Markets

From such relatively simple transactions, the next phase could be developed— broadening the mix of products purchased to include related lines from additional factories and expanding the range of exports to those factories. In the case of the Balkan furniture factory, the U.S. exporter now has a cash market for a larger volume of veneers, lacquers, sandpaper, and glues as well as wood-processing machinery. This increases the number of exporters whom we can service, in markets that may be totally new for them. In addition, the U.S. furniture buyer is now ready, willing, and able to buy in other countries where our client/exporters face countertrade or offset obligations. In fact, the company has since increased its furniture imports sevenfold to $5.0 million. In the process, it has also created counterpurchase rights of roughly half that amount. Thus it has created a market for U.S. exports of $2.5 million. The U.S. exports that the purchases facilitate for our exporter of supplies now include a number of other furniture-related products that are used to make the product that the U.S. importer buys back.

Structuring and Financing the Counterpurchase

A bank's advisory role in the structuring of transactions will frequently evolve into assessing, managing, and laying off the related credit, political, and performance risks associated with foreign transactions. These additional services permit us to finance the transaction(s) whenever the credit risks can be acceptably mitigated.

For example, our furniture importer buys from the Balkans on a ninety-day open account and sells back on a sixty-day open account. Therefore, he has a net thirty-day credit and owes the factory more than is owed to him. If the Balkans fall behind on their payments, the importer holds up his payments; this is clearly a very simple means of limiting credit risk.

The exporter also can discount or refinance the receivables by:

1. Asking a bank for short-term finance. However, banks generally will not finance credits in the Balkans unless there is an acceptable local bank guarantee or letter of credit with FCIA (Foreign Credit Insurance Association) insurance covering the letter of credit or private insurance. Additionally, the bank must be willing to take on incremental credit exposure in the importing country under most insurance programs.

2. Asking a factor to discount or buy the receivables. However, the factor will only do this if the receivables are insured by the FCIA or by a private insurer.

3. Asking the partner, the U.S. exporter, to sell directly to the importing factory in exchange for the furniture, which the factory will then resell to the exporter. The U.S. exporting partner could then extend longer credit terms to the furniture importer. In the process, the U.S. exporter would have assumed both the credit and collection risk. The exporter may then ask the bank to issue a standby letter of credit to support the furniture buyer's credit.

A BANK'S ROLE IN OFFSET PROGRAMS

As Willis Bussard (chapter 2) and Duke Golden (chapter 7) discussed, offset is the largest part of countertrade for U.S. companies. In helping our customers fulfill their offset obligations, we as a bank assume numerous creative roles involving both entrepreneurial and financial functions. To service the commercial portions of offset programs, banks are being asked to help their clients to:

- Expand exports from the offset country
- Attract investment and technology in joint ventures that increase local employment and develop depressed areas
- Expand the market for local services such as shipping, insurance, tourism, and even movie/advertising production services
- Finance subcontractor's investment in the direct or coproduction portions of the offset programs.

To respond to these requests, a bank can draw upon its corporate relationships, financial product expertise, and global network.

1. It will identify buyers for the offset country's exports. For example, regarding our earlier example of the furniture importer, that party now also plans to purchase from another offset country (Canada). Our bank is now screening potential partners who need the offset credits to be generated by his purchases. In another case, an importer of Chinese silks and fabrics with excellent long-term family relationships in China has been linked· with a U.S. exporter facing a unique offset requirement in the host country. The textile merchant's relationships significantly facilitated the necessary approvals for an innovative joint venture that will undertake to liquidate the offset obligation over a long term.

2. The bank will provide inventory and account-receivables financing and factoring for the medium-sized importers of products offered by the offset country. The importers always need longer credit terms to offer their customers and inventory financing to support the larger volumes of purchases. The merchandise, receivables, and other tangible assets serve as the bank's collateral for this ''asset-based'' financing. Since the asset-based or commercial finance units within banks deal with the middle-market importers, they are good sources of additional importers that can be brought to participation in an offset program.

3. The bank will use export credit and insurance programs within the offset country to package project export financing. The Canadian Export Development Corporation, for example, can be used to support project exports from Canada in fulfillment of major offset programs. Also, one of the aerospace firms that has obligations in Finland and Austria approached us to work with their official credit agencies to help promote project exports. We will be seeing more of this out of South Korea too—from the Korean Export-Import Bank.

4. The bank will identify and encourage potential investors for joint ventures. Banks have been asked to identify potential investors for the economically depressed regions in Canada, provinces in the Peoples Republic of China, Yugoslavia, Spain, Portugal, and Saudi Arabia, among other countries. Business and trade-development groups such as the University of South Carolina could be good partners with banks and U.S. exporters in identifying, advising, and facilitating investments in offset countries.

5. The bank will establish procedures within host countries for monitoring and recording compliance with offset requirements. Modifying the concept of

International Trade Certificates (ITC) developed by the First National Bank of Boston and General Foods (which Paul Boliek discusses in chapter 13) and using such certificates within the framework of an offset program to encompass all of the offset activities, including trade, banks can create a mechanism to facilitate, record, monitor, and evidence the fulfillment of offset program obligations. Basically, the ITC performs the role of money: it transfers value, provides a unit of account, and creates a store of value.

6. The bank will identify, formulate, and structure new uses for local currencies, such as for corporate R&D, tourist promotion, sales conferences, and academic exchanges. The University of South Carolina, for example, could accept corporate gifts or funding in soft currencies to support its student and program exchanges with foreign universities or research organizations. This technical exchange builds the skills of the host country's academic/technical personnel and conceivably could be credited to offset programs.

Each offset program is unique. Creative things have been done in offset: any program that uses local services or goods and provides value is potentially negotiable for offset credit. A bank's support services must be fashioned into a multiservice package tailor-made to the needs, capabilities, and structure of the offset country. Financial expertise inspired by creative realism will be the hallmarks of banking offsets for the foreseeable future.

10

Legal Aspects of Countertrade

THOMAS B. McVEY

IS COUNTERTRADE THE ANSWER?

Before beginning an examination of legal issues, there are several general observations to be made. As other authors have noted, countertrade should be used when cash and normal credit transactions are not feasible or when competitive conditions require it. Countertrade is not generally the ideal. Yet from my perspective as an independent advisor, I frequently see firms attempting to make countertrades in many instances when it may not be necessary, where there is other financing available. The scenario is always the same: the firm bids on a project in an overseas country. The foreign host government accepts its bid, indicating that the company will get the contract if it can come up with the financing. The firm goes to its lead bank, which refuses to finance the sale. The firm then automatically presumes that there is no financing available, that it is not going to be able to get any financing and is going to have to countertrade.

In many cases there are other ways to finance a deal. It is not always easy to finance outside of the normal U.S. trade finance patterns, but in certain instances there are options to barter that American firms tend to overlook. For instance, other banks may have an appetite for a particular type of risk in which your bank is not interested now. Or private export-credit insurance may be available. (The frequency with which we encounter American exporters and their financial advisors who are not fully aware of the benefits of private export-credit insurance is surprising.) Public credit and insurance may be available from the Export-Import Bank, FCIA, and the Commodity Credit Corporation. Also, if a firm has an overseas subsidiary, it might have access to a foreign agency.

Do not assume that a refusal from either your bank or any of these agencies is necessarily absolute. Persistent companies are often rewarded. For example, simply because the Export-Import Bank declines your loan request does not necessarily mean that your options at Eximbank are closed. The Export-Import Bank and other federal financial agencies can be lobbied like other federal offices.

Mixed credits are coming into focus as well. Other government agencies, such as the Agency for International Development, Overseas Private Investment Corporation, and the Bureau of Private Enterprise, although not trade-finance organizations, may be able in some instances to make financing available.

Explore all feasible financing options. Countertrade may or may not be the best alternative despite the initial impression.

LEGAL CONSIDERATIONS IN COUNTERTRADE

If you decide to explore the feasibility of countertrade, do not fail to consider carefully the legal issues involved. It is my experience that managers commonly are not interested in the legal issues that (they feel) only slow down the deal. They consider that legal considerations are not their job but the job of their company's lawyer. The reality is that there are some very serious legal issues involved. You would do well to at least have familiarity with some of the more important of them.

There are no federal laws that specifically address the issue of whether countertrade is legal or illegal. Legal issues can arise, however, in some of the many components of the individual countertrade transaction. Unless a company is aware of them in advance, these components can take firms by surprise when it may be too late.

The four major areas of legal concern are (1) import-relief laws, (2) federal regulations pertaining to specific import-product areas, (3) customs laws and (4) antitrust laws. These laws almost always involve the import of countertraded goods (i.e., the purchase side of the deal) rather than the export side. However, on the export side, a company should be sensitive to U.S. embargoes with certain countries. Exporters of technical equipment must always be wary of U.S. laws; Duke Golden commented on this in chapter 7.

Import-Relief Laws

The most troublesome legal area is that of the import-relief laws. These laws are the series of federal trade laws that are designed to restrict imports in certain situations. For example, the antidumping laws and the escape clause provide that if goods are imported at a price that is artificially low (for example, below cost, as in the case of the dumping laws) or if you otherwise seriously injure a domestic industry with imports, duties will be imposed or the imports restricted or prohibited under import quotas.

These laws apply to all imports, not just to the import of countertraded goods.

However, they are particularly important in countertrade because of the tendency of U.S. firms in countertrade deals to import products that are in excess on the world markets or offered at below current market price. In essence, these goods are the natural target of import-relief proceedings.

The problems with the import-relief laws would be as follows: if a firm agrees to purchase any import or countertraded product and an antidumping action is later initiated, this could interfere with the import. No one would go to jail, but it could increase the landed costs or cause one to lose a buyer.

Let me give you an example of how it might work. You sell a steel plant or the components or raw materials that go into the plant to a foreign-government-owned steel company. You agreed to buy an equivalent dollar amount of steel out of that plant over a period (for example, one shipment a month for three years) for $100 a ton. You may already have a buyer in the United States who will buy that steel from you at $100 a ton. After the first three months of the transaction, an import-relief proceeding or antidumping proceeding is commenced by the U.S. steel industry. As a result of the proceedings, import-relief duties of $25 a ton are imposed. You now are purchasing steel for $100 plus $25 in import duty. Your landed price is $125; yet you are still selling to the buyer at $100. Obviously, you may be exposed to dramatic losses, or you will lose your buyer. As a result, you would be long in steel in a weak market.

A number of countertrade transactions have thus far been challenged under the import-relief laws, including the famous anhydrous ammonia deal between Occidental Petroleum and the Soviet Union. Occidental's imports of ammonia were challenged under section 406 of the Trade Act of 1974. There was also an antidumping action in connection with a countertrade deal involving Hungarian truck-trailer axles a couple of years ago. In a recent countervailing-duty case involving textiles from Indonesia, countertrade was alleged to be a form of government subsidy, remedial by a countervailing duty. Currently pending before the International Trade Commission are a series of import-relief actions, including steel cases, tires, fish, roses, chemicals, and batteries. The list is very long.

What steps can you take to avoid import-relief problems? It is impossible to determine in advance if there will be an import-relief action initiated in a year, two years, or three years from now. But there are some recommendations for minimizing the risk in this situation.

Do not unnecessarily publicize your transaction. You have no obligation to frighten the affected industry. The impact of your imports may not be sufficient to draw attention if you remain silent. However, even a relatively small action may draw negative reaction in order to set a precedent and to deter others.

Another recommendation for protecting yourself against import-relief-law problems is to try to negotiate an option for a change of products into the contract before signing. Perhaps you can substitute importable aluminum and other types of metal or another type of commodity. A second possibility is that an import-relief proceeding can be interpreted as part of the action that is beyond the control of the parties—a force majeure. This may relieve you of an obligation either to import that particular commodity or to countertrade in general.

The most frequently suggested recommendation is to sell the counterpurchased goods to a trading company to be sold offshore. If a firm is taking steel out of Brazil, it may avoid potential problems by not bringing it to the United States. It could, however, be sold to a trading company, ideally at the point of origin. Let it worry about the import-relief actions and some of the other problems that I will discuss. Several of the authors in this book will address this issue of trading companies and other types of facilitators (see part V).

If the steel is sold directly to an end user (for example, some industrial manufacturing firm), the counterpurchaser should try to sell to the firm offshore— let it have the import risk. But if your company does sell to a firm offshore, do not let it force majeure the import-relief problem against you. Try to pass that risk to it also.

It is possible that the import relief and other types of legal actions may be insurable. Depending on the underwriter, that option should be examined as well.

Specific Product Regulations

The second area of legal concern involves regulations that pertain to specific commodities. These are the day-to-day regulations normally found in most industries. (Examples include the labeling, packaging, and health requirements in the food industry; the environmental laws in the chemical industry; and safety requirements in the consumer goods area. As you may have noticed in some of the chapters, food items, chemicals, and consumer goods are very common types of products brought back pursuant to countertrade requirements.)

These types of risks apply to such commodities in general for sale in the United States. They do not apply only to imported commodities or to counter-traded commodities. If your company is in a business that is affected, these laws are a nuisance, but you know how to deal with them, since it is your industry. But if that industry is new to your company (e.g., if you're importing chemicals for the first time), it can be very dangerous.

If you are importing goods pursuant to a countertrade arrangement, you are responsible under these laws and do run a risk of running afoul of some of the regulatory requirements if you are not familiar with the industry.

I was once asked to look at what the federal regulatory requirements would be for the import of red mullet, which is a type of fish, from the African nation of Senegal. There were requirements of the U.S. Customs Service (e.g., duties plus packaging and bonding requirements). There was a Food and Drug Administration (FDA) requirement regarding imported food products for health and sanitation reasons. There were labeling requirements including ingredients, name and address of the shipper, and weight. The Fish and Wildlife Administration checks to see whether the product is on the endangered species list; there is a

U.S. endangered species list and an international endangered-species-convention list. The Latin name of the fish is needed, and they recommend sending a sample.

The Department of Agriculture only deals with live plants and animals. But the Department of Agriculture indicated that since this product was going to be packed in straw, and since insects are frequently found in the straw, they had to inspect the packing material too.

These are just the federal laws. There could be state and local laws involved, depending on your commodity. You could avoid these laws by selling to another country, but you may well encounter similar laws there. The moral is to deal with specialists if your counterpurchase involves products with which you are unfamiliar. This may be another reason for considering the use of an international trading company.

U.S. Customs Regulations

The third area involves the U.S. Customs Service. Customs has announced that it is going to scrutinize barter transactions very carefully to make sure that the value of imported commodities is accurately reflected for purposes of collecting the full amount of duty owed.

In a ''pure'' barter situation, you literally exchange goods with no currency, with no documentation about dollar amounts, and with no currency-related instruments or mechanisms such as escrow accounts. If you ever are involved in this type of deal, be sure to keep careful records of the value of the commodity that you are exporting, because the records are likely to be used to calculate the value of the commodities being imported for purposes of calculating duty payment. This would be in the event of ad valorem duties by the Customs Service.

Antitrust Regulations

The fourth area is the antitrust area. This is currently a very hazy but potentially very explosive area in the countertrade field. Antitrust laws in a countertrade context deal with a practice called ''reciprocity,'' the requirement that if I buy from you, you must buy from me. Reciprocity can clearly be against the law in domestic commerce in many instances where there is competitive injury. The courts have just not addressed the question of reciprocity in the international context. There have been no cases fully litigated on this issue. It is an unsettled question, and time will tell what the jurisprudential wisdom is about international reciprocal dealing.

There are other practices that could raise antitrust issues as well. Sales below cost, if resulting in sufficient competitive injury, could violate the antitrust laws. For example, if you are bringing shoes into the United States and injure another party in the shoe business to a significant extent, that could create an antitrust problem. Forcing your contractors to eat some of the countertraded goods that you are taking back could also create some problems. Alleged predatory practices are also under question: if you have a very large company and control a substantial part of the market, to the extent that you get involved in moving things below cost or at a discount, the antitrust issues may arise. As countertrade becomes more highly visible in the business community, there will be more heard about the antitrust side of the business. Not even the antitrust provisions of the Export Trading Company Act will fully insulate you from some of these antitrust problems.

LESSONS LEARNED

Something else that lawyers do in these deals besides trying to tell you why you cannot make the deal is to help structure the deal plus help negotiate and develop the commercial considerations. I have identified a number of lessons that U.S. firms have learned.

Lesson Number One

Try to separate your sales obligation from your purchase obligation to as great an extent as possible. If you look closely at the different types of countertrade transactions, you will see that most transactions involve parallel sales transactions: they are really nothing more than two separate sales transactions linked in some form to each other in a reciprocal fashion. I sell the radar to you; you pay me in dollars, frequently under a letter of credit in normal commerce. In return, you sell the steel to me, and I pay you in dollars. These events may occur simultaneously or later in time.

Private firms have learned that it is often desirable to structure the countertrade transaction as if the sale from the private firm to the sovereign government, the *primary* sale, and the sale from the government back to the private firm, the *secondary* sale, are two entirely separate events.

In addition, as Christopher Korth mentioned in chapter 1, separation of the contracting agreement, in many cases, makes financing and insuring the deals somewhat easier. As a result, you most likely want to try to get (1) separate contract documents for both the primary and the secondary agreement; (2) separate finance, insurance, and penalty provisions; (3) no reference in the first agreement to the obligation in the second agreement; and (4) no linking or cross-referencing of these separate obligations to the extent possible.

The sovereign government, on the other hand, will want the obligations linked as closely as possible. It is aware that the only reason you are buying its products is because it is buying your products. It will want to use one agreement or, if there are two agreements, have them cross-referenced in as many instances as possible and most likely use the penalty procedure in the secondary set of contracts.

As a compromise, parties in a counterpurchase/countersales transaction frequently end up with two separate sales documents cross-linked by a side agreement or protocol with a penalty provision in the secondary sales agreement.

Lesson Number Two

In structuring an agreement, be careful how your secondary sales contract is drafted. The primary sales contract generally is straightforward because it uses the terms that are normally employed in a standard export contract of the commodity. The wording of the secondary contract is trickier. There is a long list of clauses that I think should be included.

1. *Transfer Clause*: It is desirable to include a clause in the second agreement that allows that the private firm, when it is counterpurchasing, will be free to transfer that obligation to another party, such as a trading company, rather than having to buy the product directly. Instead of buying the products back, a company could have a buyer in place on a back-to-back basis so that the counterpurchasing company is in the title chain for as short a period as possible. It is preferable not even to be placed in the title chain but to bring in a buyer to purchase in your stead, if possible. It may take some doing to get the sovereign government to agree to that. You want to try to remove yourself from the chain of title to as great an extent as possible.

2. *Cross-Cancellation Clause*: It is also desirable to enclose a clause that provides that in the event the primary contract is cancelled, the secondary contract is cancelled also.

3. *Freedom-of-Resale Clause*: Another provision should provide that there are no restrictions on the resale of the product that is counterpurchased. The sovereign government wants to make sure that it controls where this material is sold to protect its existing market interests in that material.

4. *Independent-Penalty Clause*: The counterpurchaser will also want a provision that indicates that the payment by him of a penalty under the secondary contract would not interfere in any way with any of his rights to be paid under the primary contract.

Lesson Number Three

With barter transactions, a separate set of technical and commercial problems arise since there is theoretically no currency in the deal. The security normally provided by a letter of credit is eliminated. The mechanics of exchanging goods at different times are problematic, and since the goods bartered are frequently surplus products that otherwise are hard to sell, there may well be quality-control problems.

U.S. firms have devised a number of methods to assist in resolving these kinds of problems, including the use of escrow accounts, reciprocal standby letters of credit, and performance guarantees. Basically, some money is introduced into the deal somewhere as the safety net, and if one of the parties fails, the money is available as protection. Thus even in the barter context, where the deal is more complicated, it can be done safely.

In conclusion, countertrade can be tricky. It can be managed from a technical perspective. My advice is to be cautious, to seek and listen to the suggestions of other more experienced managers, but, in the final analysis, to use your good common sense.

11

Operational Aspects of Countertrade

RICHARD V. L. COOPER

Here in the United States we are witnessing a dramatic change in the corporate attitude and knowledge of countertrade. In the past, many companies naively have entered into countertrade contracts without the aid of appropriate expert advice. In one case, for example, a telephone manufacturer negotiated a deal with Poland, and part of the contract involved a counterpurchase of some parts that would be included in the company's final product in the United States. The product was a very visible part of the final product: the rotary dial. The only difficulty was that it was produced in only three colors: shocking pink, bright orange, and chartreuse. They were useless to the company. However, this could be easily remedied by careful advance planning.

Several weeks ago my family was personally exposed to a marketing mistake. We were looking for bookcases, and the ones we found looked very nice, so we ordered them. When they arrived at the house they came disassembled, like so much furniture today. Assembling furniture is not generally very complicated—certainly not bookcases. But there was one minor problem: the instructions were written in Serbo-Croatian!

COUNTERTRADE IN THE 1980s

American companies are going to find that requirements to accept barter in exchange for their sales are increasingly frequent in the coming years. Fortunately, there is a much higher degree of awareness and sophistication and a much wider range of third-party expertise to aid the counterpurchaser; some of these types of expertise are discussed elsewhere in this book.

American companies often find countertrade requirements to be serious problems. Some companies simply forego such sales and profits. Even worse, some
companies enter into ill-conceived countertrade deals. This can mean large losses
from goods that are not moved, or it can mean penalties for failing to meet a
counterpurchase obligation. Furthermore, what is too often forgotten is that poor
contract performance can lose *future* contracts as well. How well a company
does today in satisfying its countertrade and offset obligations, just as with any
other business obligation, can have a major effect on the kind of business that
it can do next year and the year after.

The barter situations that we as consultants encounter are of two kinds: those
where the countertrade arrangement has already been agreed to and, the preferred
variety, those in which we become involved before the deal has been finalized.
There is often not much that we can do in the former case. Often we can only
try to limit the damage. There may be some room for further negotiation, but
the base terms of the contract have been set.

Much more fruitful from a company's point of view is to plan very seriously
and with expert counsel from the beginning. There are three key issues that need
to be addressed: (1) knowing when to bid, (2) knowing how to bid, and (3)
knowing how to perform.

Those three are interrelated issues, since how well you can perform is going
to greatly affect what situations you want to bid on. If you have a very capable
organization, you will be willing to undertake more bids. Conversely, if you
are a neophyte in the area, you may want to enter gradually into deals that are
simpler.

Knowing When To Bid

Very often American exporters will feel that governments that are prospective
buyers are very unreasonable in terms of what they expect in countertrade. What
is unreasonable and what is a firm's willingness to enter into those arrangements
will depend upon the firm's resources and capabilities.

There are three options open to a company when countries appear to be
unreasonable. First, you may be able to get them to negotiate down to something
that is more manageable. Failing that, you can attempt to adjust your price
accordingly; Willis Bussard stressed in chapter 2 the importance of incorporating
satisfactory pricing into countertrade deals. The third option is simply to walk
away from an unacceptable deal. If the proposed arrangements are not satisfactory, it is unwise to proceed. Many companies punish themselves when they are
willing to accept a deal at any price.

Knowing How To Bid

There are a number of approaches or options available in bidding. Direct offset
is very often dictated by certain large military contracts or other large projects.

Straight barter, although relatively rare in corporate barter, is feasible in some instances.

Counterpurchase is much more common; historically, it is used more with commodities, low-grade industrial products, and some consumer products. But counterpurchases are not going to be as large a share of countertrade in the future as today. The commodity markets have really been saturated to a large extent, and the prices have been driven down by one to another, but people are beginning to recognize this. There just is not the market today for the low-grade industrial products. What will happen instead is that companies can begin to work with the producers of low-grade industrial products to upgrade the quality. That is going to be one of the important areas where you, as part of countertrade, can really work with the steel company or the ballbearing company to help it upgrade.

As James Barkas noted in chapter 9, tourism, advertising, and movie making are increasingly popular arrangements. Compensation buy-back agreements are also going to be around, but they are going to be very project-specific.

The things that really will change and be emphasized more in the future are project or industrial development. The buying countries are becoming more sophisticated in what they expect from countertrade. They are beginning to realize now that often the oil, or the cotton, or the minerals that they are selling would have been sold anyway and very often at a similar price and, in some cases, even at a higher price. They want to use countertrade to foster their industrial development. Thus they are looking to the more experienced Western firms to help them upgrade their industry and infrastructure. Developing countries, in particular, are eager to acquire food-processing technology. For example, there is a fairly good business in tomato-paste plants. Interestingly, the most difficult part of one particular deal has been to line up the necessary supply of tomatoes, since very often the smaller countries have many small farms; processors generally prefer a few large producers.

Shrimp farms are also becoming very popular. They are another good project to consider in developing countries with attractive locations along the coast, such as Greece, Turkey, much of Central America, and the Caribbean islands, where growing conditions are good. Projects of this sort are going to be an important area for countertrade. These projects are very suitable to smaller countertrade contracts (i.e., those that are measured in the millions or tens of millions of dollars as opposed to those that are measured in the hundreds of millions or billions of dollars).

Grander-scale industrial developments are also becoming more prominent; the best example to date is one that was just recently announced, the Saudi procurement of what is known as the "Peace Shield." This is the command-control communication system that they have been developing for some time. They just announced the winning bidder, Boeing, which has agreed to reinvest about $1 billion dollars in Saudi Arabia. The Saudis are worried about their economy after oil depletion begins. They want to develop a technologically sophisticated industry.

General Motors is perhaps trying to do something even more ambitious in Egypt, to help it develop a full-scale automobile industry—including many parts suppliers.

One final thing in this area of knowing how to bid that is terribly important is to think about how to package deals. It used to be that people would talk about a counterpurchase program, and you would look at just what things you would select from the list. Financing is much more important, so it is not just the particular product. The deal may be combining counterpurchase and compensation and financing. A company needs to think about how to package an entire deal—not just focus on one narrow aspect of the countertrade program.

Knowing How To Perform

One of the first choices a company faces is how to approach these deals organizationally. There are many approaches, from one extreme of building the entire function in-house to the other extreme of handing it off entirely to third parties. There has been tremendous improvement in the quality of the third parties available. There are even a number of smaller firms that have emerged that are good.

There are four classes of organizations that could offer a broad-scale countertrade support activity. One is clearly the Japanese trading companies, which have a tremendous worldwide capability. Willis Bussard's study (chapter 2) indicated that they are not yet widely used by U.S. firms, but they will likely become more prominent in the future. A second group comprises some of the major multinationals. Third are the major international banks. Fourth are the accounting firms and consulting firms. Each group has its own strengths but also some fairly glaring weaknesses. How well each deals with those weaknesses will determine the role it can play in barter. The banks may enter the barter field in a major way. The problem that banks encounter is that the person most often out in their foreign office is a banker, not a trader; a traditional banker will have difficulty understanding the nuances of structuring barter deals. The same thing is true with the accounting firms. The guy that is in our foreign office is traditionally an accountant, not a trader or countertrader. Nevertheless, the resources that the banks and accounting or consulting firms have with their worldwide networks offer potential for development.

For most companies, my recommendation is to structure themselves organizationally somewhere between the do-it-all-yourself approach and the hand-it-all-over approach. The lawyers, the bankers, and the consultants should be brought in when their skills are appropriate, but in-house capability should be used where it exists.

In conclusion, two key issues for successful countertrade are (1) to get executives involved early (Stephen Crain's experiences (chapter 8) shed significant light on the importance of this) and (2) to plan early. This need not be an elaborate process, but it does mean thinking through the problems, thinking through the solutions, and thinking through the opportunities at an early stage.

12

Strategic Planning for Countertrade

MARY JANE IAIA-McPHEE AND SETH MAEROWITZ

The purpose of this presentation is to introduce and apply the concept of strategic planning to countertrade. Today many corporations view countertrade as a necessary evil that can only be dealt with on a case-by-case basis. By making it an integral part of a company's planning process, the barriers presented by countertrade can often be overcome and used to strengthen a company's overall market position. This chapter presents general guidelines on how to determine and define an effective strategic approach for countertrade.

CORPORATE COUNTERTRADE STRATEGY

The development of a corporate countertrade strategy involves four basic steps: (1) defining the countertrade objectives of the company; (2) analyzing market potential in foreign markets; (3) developing a market-specific countertrade approach; and (4) implementing that strategy. The fourth step is described lucidly in other chapters in this book. This section, therefore, focuses on steps 1, 2, and 3. Our goal is not to provide a detailed methodology for strategic planning in this area but instead to introduce a general framework that can be applied across a broad spectrum of industries and markets.

Step 1: Define Countertrade Objectives

When we speak about defining countertrade objectives, we are asking the question, "What is a company really looking for when it engages in countertrade?" A company that is already active in exporting to less-developed countries

EXHIBIT 12.1

DEFINE OBJECTIVES

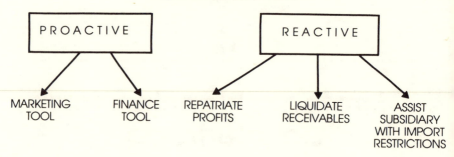

or one with subsidiaries that have problems repatriating profits may find that countertrade offers new options for reaching those markets or freeing those funds. Two approaches are possible in setting objectives—proactive and reactive. In the *reactive approach*, a specific goal is set, usually based on the need to solve an already identified problem (Exhibit 12.1). This type of goal can involve actions such as repatriating profits, liquidating receivables, and assisting subsidiaries with import restrictions.

In the *proactive approach*, CT is viewed as a marketing or finance tool for maintaining and accessing new markets that otherwise would be closed. The focus of this chapter is on using countertrade as a proactive marketing tool—or how it can be used as an integrated part of a company's global marketing plan in order to be prepared for countertrade opportunities or requirements rather than merely responding to them.

Step 2: Analyzing Market Potential in Foreign Markets

The first step in analyzing market potential involves identifying the company's key foreign markets. This analysis requires answers to a number of key questions. Where are the customers located? In which countries is the company interested in doing business? Which of those markets are most likely to be profitable? What will be the cost of entering those markets? In which of those markets can countertrade be used effectively? Which of those countries are going to require countertrade? Which countries should be ignored because of the difficult countertrade regulations or the company's lack of resources?

The answers begin with data gathered from the International Monetary Fund, from the World Bank, or from specific government agencies in the countries being examined. The data give an understanding of what the growth potential is in different markets, which industries are growing, and what their needs might be as well as assisting the company in deciding how it might go about responding to these needs. Once the data have been gathered, they should be supplemented and refined through interviews with people who have personal experience in those countries and, if possible, through visits to the actual local markets.

The next task is to identify those markets that have the greatest profit potential, to assess what the competition is doing, and to determine whether any niche or "opportunity" gap remains unfilled. If a promising niche is identified, the company must then decide how to position the product to compete effectively, as well as to determine the market size thresholds that are necessary to make it viable. Trade magazines and newspapers can often be helpful in terms of analyzing the competition and evaluating the best way to position a product. Competitor advertising and attendance at trade fairs also are useful sources on how products are being priced and promoted.

Countertrade is not important in all markets. Thus it is important at this point to focus on those markets that are going to require countertrade. An understanding is needed of the import priorities attached to the product in various countries. In Venezuela or Ecuador, for instance, if a Western product is high on its import-priorities list, countertrade is likely to be less of a problem than it would be if the product were lower in priority for the country. Another useful piece of information is what countertrade arrangements are being favored by the country itself. For instance, Mexico at this time is favoring nontraditional exports or exports of traditional products to nontraditional markets. The Mexicans look very favorably on a firm that is willing to help them modify production of their products to become more saleable on the world market.

The steps involved in analyzing countertrade market potential may be summed up as follows (Exhibit 12.2):

1. *The identification of world markets*

   a. Identify opportunities.
   b. Screen and refine opportunities.
   c. Define markets.

2. *The isolation of profitable potential markets*

   a. Identify entry barriers and competition.
   b. Decide how to position products.
   c. Determine market-size threshold.

3. *The identification of viable countertrade markets*

   a. Establish the import priority of the product.
   b. Assess countertrade and other regulations.
   c. Identify markets and technologies the less-developed country (LDC) seeks to develop.

This preparatory work should provide a reasonable basis for selecting specific countertrade policies that will include the least cost for market entry and that will be compatible with corporate global strategies for the allocation of its re-

EXHIBIT 12.2

ANALYSIS OF CT MARKET POTENTIAL

P R O A C T I V E   S T R A T E G Y

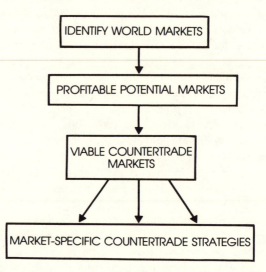

sources. The procedure thus involves correlating market needs with corporate resources and objectives and then applying the chosen strategies for coping with countertrade commitments in the markets in which the company chooses to operate.

Step 3: Developing a Countertrade Strategy for Each Market

Three substrategies can be considered (Exhibit 12.3). The first is a *global sourcing strategy*: What can be exported from the country under consideration (i.e., the source of the goods)? The second is a *global distribution strategy*: How can our existing distribution network take either products that are already being used or different products? Finally, the market may call for use of an *industrial development strategy* if plans call for the company to be directly involved in the country for a long time: Are we willing to make the extensive commitment that might be required? Is the contract large enough to justify a direct investment not only in a specific product, or in a specific firm, but in the industrial development of the country itself? For example, two basic types of industrial development are those that involve either technology transfer or direct investment. Both come together very often because usually whenever technology is transferred, some investment is needed. In some cases, a standard technology,

EXHIBIT 12.3

DEVELOPING MARKET-SPECIFIC CT STRATEGIES: 1

a technology that is not proprietary, can be used so that information is not given out that might help create a new competitor.

Global Sourcing Strategy: There are four types of global sourcing strategies that can be employed—purchasing from a foreign vendor, licensing another company to produce the product using your technology, joint-venture relationships, and 100 percent equity relationships (Exhibit 12.4). Each involves progressively greater and longer-term commitments to the country.

The development of a global sourcing strategy based on purchasing from a foreign vendor involves three steps. These steps entail evaluating the real costs of taking this particular route, the risks, and the hoped-for returns and benefits.

When sourcing is done through a foreign vendor (purchasing for internal use), the first step is to complete a purchasing audit to see what can be sourced from the country to meet in-house manufacturing and production needs. This involves coordinating many different resources in our company, but primarily it means coordinating the purchasing or materials-management group with the sales-support group. In addition, other people need to be involved not only in determining what is going to be taken out of the country and how it is going to be taken out but who will be involved in the negotiating process. The engineering staff, for example, can help determine what the product is and whether it can be reconfigured for your needs—that is, whether any design or packaging changes need to be made. The legal department should be consulted for contract negotiation, for setting up the facility, and for finalizing the arrangements. The manufacturing group determines products and quality control. It needs to be consulted about

EXHIBIT 12.4

DEVELOPING MARKET-SPECIFIC CT STRATEGIES: 2

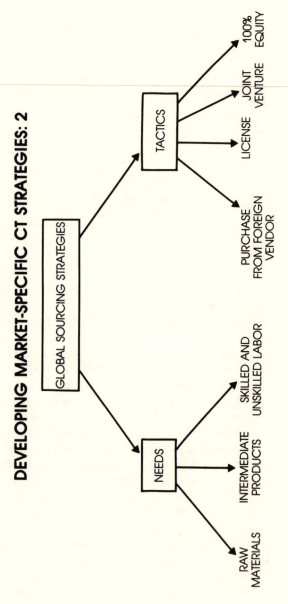

whether it can maintain an ongoing supply of products. Finally, external sources of information should be investigated—such as the U.S. government, foreign governments, freight forwarders, custom-house brokers, bankers, and customers.

After the purchasing audit, the next step requires a close examination of potential risks: delivery, quality, exchange controls, and other regulatory risks. Variability in quality is an obvious risk that needs no further amplification. Many issues are involved in delivery risk. A lot of obstacles in the delivery cycle can prevent the product from getting to port and, in turn, from being delivered to you. Talking to different political risk-insurance companies can give you a good idea about the delivery obstacles that might be encountered—the labor situation in the country and any production, warehousing, and shipment problems. During the past three or four years the American Insurance Group (AIG), as well as Lloyds, has become more active in covering political and delivery-risk aspects of countertrade transactions.

Country risk, the political climate, the foreign-exchange situation in the individual country, the creditworthiness of the company from which you would be sourcing and that of the country are other important considerations. Are they undergoing a rescheduling, and if so, at what stage are they in this process? How are regulations and different restrictions that are likely to flow out of that rescheduling going to affect you? For example, not too long ago in Mexico, the whole situation of oil exports changed dramatically as oil became encumbered by the International Monetary Fund (IMF) and it was no longer possible for oil to be used in certain countertrade situations.

Once you have ascertained that a risk is present, the next step is to decide how to manage that risk. Depending on the type or types of risk encountered you might have your engineering staff conduct an on-site examination of the suppliers or take steps to hedge the foreign-exchange risk and, if a commodity is being taken out in raw-material form, the commodity risk as well. Another way to manage risk is to source through multiple channels rather than just through one source in the country. However, this will often involve setting up many linkage agreements through various government authorities to insure credit is provided for the exports in exchange for new import permits.

The next step is to look at the real costs involved—both tangible and intangible (Exhibit 12.5). On the intangible side are all of the efforts that go into actually finding that product that you are going to source. Also included is an evaluation of the quality of the product and the supplier's ability to maintain an ongoing supply of the product. Other intangible costs include the efforts that subsequently go into negotiating the supply contract, evaluating the supply contract, and renewing it from time to time. Those are intangible costs that still have to be factored and considered in weighting the cost and benefit of a global sourcing strategy.

The tangible costs are far easier to identify—price, forecasting of price fluctuations, freight and shipment costs, warehousing, packaging, documentation, and tariffs. All are well understood with the possible exception of finance costs

EXHIBIT 12.5

REAL COSTS

INTANGIBLE	TANGIBLE
PRODUCT RESEARCH	PRODUCT PRICE
QUALITY CONTROL	FREIGHT & SHIPMENT
CONTRACT NEGOTIATION & EVALUATION	WAREHOUSING
MANAGING ON-GOING SUPPLY	PACKAGING
	DOCUMENTATION
	TARIFFS
	FINANCE

in which we have also included insurance. The various financing vehicles used to support countertrade have been discussed at length in chapters 9 and 13 in this book and will not be expanded upon here.

Having looked at the risks and having attempted to manage them and having looked at the costs, the next task is to weigh them in light of the sales revenue of the export product. Is it a marginal export? Is it an important or strategic product? Is this a long-term relationship that could be developed? All of these factors will weigh against unusual costs or unusual risks to balance out the equation. The returns and benefits should also be viewed in terms of the diversification of sources of supply. Diversification could provide additional leverage with traditional suppliers in obtaining better prices.

A Case Study

A case study of how one company has actually used the global sourcing strategy outlined above as a proactive marketing tool may be illustrative. This particular pharmaceutical company recognized that Brazil represented a strong potential market for the company over the long term. It also knew that the Brazilians were seeking to expand export markets for specific products. The company wanted to focus on those products and try to link them both to assist its subsidiary in overcoming import restrictions and to enable the parent company to directly export to Brazil without going through all of the problems and delays of securing import permits.

The company examined its in-house purchasing capabilities and found that there was a great deal of flexibility. It had been sourcing many products from Western Europe and from the United States that could have been sourced from Brazil. A group of products was identified that might be appropriate; ultimately, they selected glass vials as the product that would be bought from Brazil. Glass vials are used in the company's in-house production but are also sold through an extensive distributorship network in Latin and Central America; the company would thus be able to dispose of any excess supplies of glass vials that it did not need to use in its in-house manufacturing facilities.

Having identified the exact product it wanted to take out, the pharmaceutical company next examined the delivery risks and costs and established a sourcing relationship for this purpose with a Brazilian supplier. The company then went to the Foreign Trade Organization (FTO) to obtain a linkage agreement. The pharmaceutical company agreed to take out certain quantities of glass vials. The FTO agreed that the payments would be earmarked to pay the company for the products that it would be exporting to Brazil. The linkage agreement also did assist the multinational's subsidiary in Brazil in overcoming certain of the import-licensing restrictions imposed by Brazil.

Every time there is a shipment of glass vials, purchase orders are sent to the FTO as evidence that the contract has been operating smoothly, so that hard currency can be released and the multinational company ultimately paid. Some of the vials are being used internally. The others are being sold through the multinational's South and Central American marketing network.

CONCLUSIONS

The first step in developing a strategic planning process for a company is to define the company's objectives. First, it must decide whether it is a proactive or a reactive countertrader and obtain the support and the commitment of senior management. Second, it must analyze countertrade in the context of the global market to determine which markets are promising. Countertrade is nothing more than another entry barrier in the international marketplace. Third, it must identify the resources it has to meet these objectives. Much planning and marketing talent in multinationals already is devoted to international marketing. That talent should be involved in this process. Fourth, the company must develop a specific strategy for each market and match those strategies with in-house capabilities. The results of that matching will in turn dictate whether it should pursue an industrial development strategy, a global sourcing strategy, or a global distribution strategy. If a decision is made to pursue a global sourcing strategy, the first step is to do a purchasing audit, product research, and a supplier evaluation. Then risk, cost, and return need to be evaluated.

The potential is enormous for those who know the rules of the game in advance and plan their game strategy well. Participants who plan carefully will enjoy a competitive edge and be able to exert greater control over the rules and hence the ultimate outcome of the countertrade game.

13

International Trading Certificates

PAUL E. BOLIEK

The concept of international trading certificates (ITC) was originated by Hector Caram-Andruet, president of General Foods Trading Company. We presented the concept of ITCs to a group of forty major international corporations in June 1984. The response was especially gratifying to us. Thirty-nine of the forty companies indicated that they found ITCs both attractive and potentially useful to them. We hope that you will share their enthusiasm.

INEFFICIENCIES OF COUNTERTRADE

Bilateralism

One of the most serious constraints of countertrade is that it is basically bilateral. The complexity of trying to handle countertrade on a one-on-one basis is one of the problems that prompted us to develop this concept of international trading certificates. Regardless of sophisticated refinements, barter is a very complex, time-consuming and relatively inefficient type of activity. No uniform international principles or practices seem to exist. It is a field for experts, not amateurs.

Bilaterialism commonly forces corporations to deal with products, materials, or services that are foreign to their areas of expertise and marketing know-how. This slows or aborts the trade process and increases the organizational and financial resources that are needed to accomplish satisfactory marketing results—often with a high level of risk and uncertainty.

Unstandardized Documentation

This shortcoming of bilateralism is aggravated by the nonexistence of acceptable, standardized documentation. Countertrade is generally conducted with a low level of participation by banks. Documentary links, which we usually rely upon commercial banks to supply, are, if available at all, neither standardized nor guided by uniform international principles or practices. Thus it appeared to us at General Foods that the standardization of countertrade methods and practices under reliable documentary processes that link disciplined trade intermediaries would be a major improvement in the practice of countertrade. It would be analogous to the appearance of letters of credit generations ago, which contributed greatly to the growth of international trade.

THE NATURE OF ITCs

What Is an ITC?

The *ITC* is a transferable instrument that would be issued by the exporter of goods from the country that requires countertrade for its imports. It would be issued to the importer or purchaser of the product and endorsed by the central bank (or designated commercial bank) of the country that issued it. The ITC would grant an irrevocable and marketable right to the holder of the certificate to export products to that countertrading country in exchange for hard currency.

The certificates may be restricted either as to their counterexport value, the types of products, the time frame in which they are or can be redeemed, or even the countries where they would be recognized. The ideal is to have a minimum number of restrictions in order to maximize their trading value.

One of the key characteristics of international trading certificates would be their transferability to third parties. Therein lies one of the benefits that we see in handling various types of trading activities through this system. The ITCs can be sold or exchanged.

Varieties of ITCs

ITCs will be offered in three forms:

1. An "advised" ITC involves the bank as an authenticator, notifier, and broker. No credit guarantee is provided by the bank, although it may be possible to obtain country-risk insurance from an insurance company.

2. An "advised and guaranteed" ITC involves the bank as the guarantor against nonpayment in addition to its role as authenticator, notifier, and broker.

3. A "confirmed" ITC is analogous to a confirmed letter of credit. A second bank confirms or guarantees the warranty of the first bank. Therefore, the holder of the

certificate is protected by promises of (1) the central bank, (2) the advising bank, and (3) the confirming bank.

The Role of Commercial Banks

To add a certain amount of validity to the international trading certificate, General Foods Trading Company has arranged that these certificates would be validated by an American bank. The Bank of Boston is our initial banking partner to help develop the concept in the banking community. It is prepared to handle any of these trading certificates from the standpoint of proper certification against counterfeiting, documentation, and buying or selling; in some cases the bank may even confirm (i.e., guarantee payment). The bank's role in selling the certificates would be as a broker—it would not be the buyer.

In some countries where the economic conditions are extremely difficult, it may be possible to put the value of the imports that are represented by these certificates into escrow. This is one of the cases where the bank may be willing to confirm the certificates. We are also in the process of developing an arrangement whereby these trading certificates can be insured against country risk.

Clearing System

In conjunction with the Bank of Boston, a clearing system is being developed that will eventually constitute a network of banks, trading companies, brokers, exporters, and importers that will participate in the offer and demand for international trading certificates. The Bank of Boston is positioning itself to provide ample services in connection with the search, validation, and commercialization of ITCs. General Foods Trading Company will strive to become a leading food-trading company, participating in the market as a seller and buyer of ITCs.

An Example

Exhibit 13.1 indicates basically how the ITC concept would work. The Atlantis exporter (1), which might be an exporter in a Third World country, makes a sale to the U.S. importer (2). One of the trade incentives that the exporter would offer is some percentage of the value of that sale (up to 100 percent or even more) in the form of trading certificates. These certificates are especially important in *commitment countries*—those that require a commitment from foreign exporters that it will arrange counterbalancing imports. Their validation would be guaranteed by the central bank of the issuing government (3).

The U.S. importer may or may not have a direct and immediate use for those certificates. If it happens to be an export-import house, the firm may actually redeem them for merchandise it needs. If the firm is basically an importer, it may sell these export rights (the ITCs) in the marketplace through the Bank of Boston (4). Other companies (5) that are in need of countertrade credits in order

EXHIBIT 13.1

ITC FLOW CHART

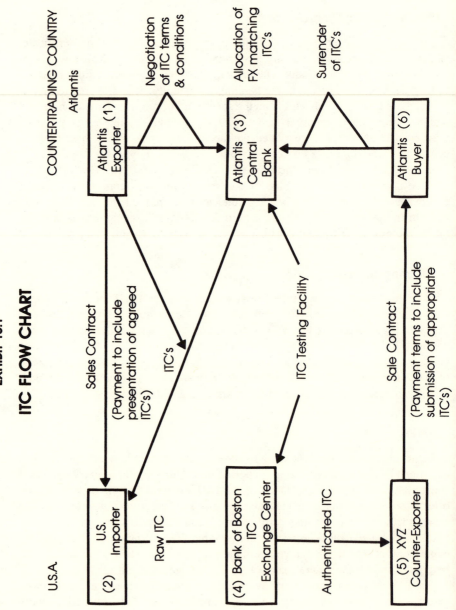

to be able to export to the commitment country can purchase these certificates to satisfy their countertrade needs. The document then moves to the buyer in the commitment country (6) and back to the central bank (3) through to the ITC exchange at the Bank of Boston (4). The counterexporter in the United States can purchase its import requirements in the form of the ITCs through the Bank of Boston; it can then use them as a replacement or equivalent of countertrade needs to sell its products back into the commitment country where the process originated.

Successful Use of ITCs

A key point to stress here is that the issuance of an ITC does not guarantee to the U.S. exporter that its sale will actually take place. It does, however, warrant that if an exporter has reached a sales agreement with a foreign-country purchaser, and if as a part of that arrangement there was a commitment to buy something from that country in countertrade, these certificates can be used to satisfy that requirement. In other words, the U.S. exporter can meet its countertrade needs through the purchase of international trade certificates, which had been previously issued by that same country as a result of some exports from that country. The central bank guarantee also warrants that foreign exchange equal to the amount of the ITC is available and will be paid upon presentation of the certificate.

The Value of ITCs

The transfer value of ITCs is determined by the marketplace—similar to the process of market valuation of commercial paper or commodity-future contracts.

A variety of factors are likely to affect the value of ITCs. Foremost is the market's perception of the value of the payment promises attached to the ITC; the credit rating of some central banks will certainly be more attractive to the market than others. The degree of restrictions on the use of the certificates will also greatly affect their value; the greater the restrictions, the less desirable the ITCs will be. The supply and demand conditions will be a major factor determining the market value of the ITCs. The demand side will be very much affected by the restrictions and the appeal of the issuer also. The exchange fees will also probably vary according to these various conditions.

At the time that the ITC is issued, the company that has purchased the products needs to negotiate for a minimum number of restrictions in its ITCs since that will improve their marketability and value. For example, in Argentina, usually we could expect the Argentine government to make ITCs valid for all imports that are in Category B, which are products that require an import license but which are not restricted totally from importation. However, if a U.S. exporter is trying to sell a product that falls in Category C, which is a totally restricted product, the ITC will do it no good. On the other hand, if it is selling a product that falls in Category B, the fact that the ITC is available is tantamount to having a guarantee of an import license.

Advantages of ITCs

One of the advantages of the international trade certificate is that it promotes exports by facilitating countertrade operations. An exporter may not, for example, be well equipped to handle countertrade on its own but for a small sum can buy the "credit" for what someone else has already bought. This mechanism facilitates the trading operation.

Another obvious advantage is that the countertrade credit (the ITC), by being reduced to a respected and acceptable documentary system, can easily be transferred from one company to another—even from one country to another. Since the certificates have been confirmed and validated through the central bank of the country of issue and perhaps also by a Western bank, the assurance that in effect the money really is there is greatly increased—somewhat analogous to a confirmed letter of credit.

Another benefit is that the certificate can be handled through the normal banking community. Many more transactions can thus be handled by a firm with a smaller organization since it does not need to worry simultaneously about its sale to the issuing country and the disposition of counterpurchased products. However, the certificate's greatest advantage is that it changes countertrade from a bilateral transaction to a multilateral transaction, and it standardizes the norms and procedures that can be used.

For the country that issues the countertrade credit, a great benefit is the certificate's advantage as an export incentive. By use of this ITC concept, the country can frequently offset some of the disadvantages that it may have in helping its customer to find a market for the commitment country's products; if that importer can sell these countertrade rights for an additional fee, that reduces its net costs and makes it easier to be competitive in the marketplace. That adds a significant amount of liquidity to the international trading community because these certificates can be readily exchanged from companies that have a surplus of trading rights to those that are badly in need.

The international trade certificate can serve as a vehicle to expand East–West and North–South trade through this transferability. It also can significantly reduce the cost of countertrade activities by permitting countertrade, in effect, to be handled by companies that are doing the things they know best. As an example, General Foods knows nothing about shoes, but it knows a lot about food; we would much rather handle the food aspects of countertrade and let some other company do the shoe transactions. ITCs will be one way of doing this.

THE ITC AS AN INTERNATIONAL INSTRUMENT

Legal Characteristics

From a legal perspective, the ITC is similar to the advise notice by a correspondent bank, notifying the terms of a letter of credit issued by another bank.

Although the ITC is not, strictly speaking, a completely negotiable instrument under section 3.104 of the U.S. Uniform Commercial Code, it does have similar characteristics and much of the legal protection of a letter of credit.

General Agreement on Tariffs and Trade (GATT)

GATT has yet to define clearly its position in regard to countertrade. (Michael Czinkota discusses this in chapter 23.) GATT's norms permit countries with balance-of-payment problems to use exceptional measures. Export-promoting techniques would clearly appear to be acceptable. The ITC is such a technique: it promotes rather than obstructs international trade by documenting the international trading rights of the holder of the certificate.

International Monetary Fund (IMF)

We believe that the IMF should welcome the development of ITCs for a number of reasons: (1) by promoting international trade through the multilateralization of countertrade; (2) by facilitating the use of goods and services as a means of payment; (3) by adding liquidity to the international monetary system; (4) by disciplining the methods and processes of countertrade and increasing the role of banks as disciplined intermediaries; (5) by facilitating the transfer of liquidity and of technology from industrial nations to less-developed ones; (6) by increasing trade and thus alleviating the recessionary pressure of import restrictions; and (7) by providing documentary evidence that will help to properly record counterexport payment commitments. All of these situations should be very positive aspects from the point of view of the IMF.

Attitude of Governments

Officials of many governments have expressed basic interest in the ITC concept. Mexico and Argentina have already approved them. I will be going to Czechoslovakia shortly for further discussions. In addition, Poland, Russia, Hungary, Brazil, Colombia, Costa Rica, and Peru are among the countries with which we have held discussions already.

The certificates are being considered as aids in some offset contracts—including some that are already in existence. The issue was first raised by CACEX and the central bank in Brazil. Brazil has a number of existing bilateral counterpurchase agreements under which it has bought much more than it has sold. To encourage the trading partners to buy more of Brazil's products, which will both satisfy Brazil's obligations and reopen its opportunities to buy more under the terms of these agreements, ITCs might be fruitful.

THE APPROPRIATENESS OF ITC's

The ITC will not be applicable in every trading situation. It does not substitute for money. It never should. If you can sell for cash, sell for cash.

The ITC is generally not useful for huge commodity-trading operations that are well established. It fits into the trading picture in the areas of incremental trade, where it helps to promote sales of new products into new markets, where some additional incentive is necessary in order to "grease the wheels." In that particular aspect, it offers many potential benefits.

Many foreign countries and also many companies are very nervous about acknowledging that they are doing countertrade. We have pointed out to them that, strictly speaking, the trading certificate is not countertrade: in fact, it is a substitute for countertrade. It is permitting a more flexible system of international trade. In effect, the system provides the same benefits as countertrade, namely, a means to permit a cash-short country to find a way to pay for desired imports through the growth and development of additional exports. To these countries and companies, we describe the ITC as a trade facilitator and not countertrade; it makes them feel more comfortable.

It is our belief that the ITCs are a revolutionary opportunity to improve the process of international countertrade. The responses we have been receiving from both corporations and governments have certainly fueled our enthusiasm.

Much still needs to be done. The ITC is a new concept. Much negotiating and educating is still needed. The format of the certificates and the mechanism of the clearing mechanism will undoubtedly evolve over time. However, a potentially revolutionary concept is developing.

PART V

FACILITATORS OF COUNTERTRADE

14

The Specialized Countertrading Company

FRANK A. OCWIEJA

At MG Services, we are often asked, "How long will this fad called countertrade or barter last?" Certainly, the sudden international credit crunch that spurred the recent growth of countertrade a few years ago subsided somewhat as world trade has begun to grow again. Now that some pundits have even announced the end of the international-debt crisis, it is easy to think that countertrade may fade away just as quickly as it appeared.

However, the expansion of countertrade has resulted in the wide introduction of a trading approach to doing business internationally, involving most notably linking two or more transactions together in order to close them. This business strategy is second nature in the commercial sectors of Europe and Japan but relatively new to industry in Canada and the United States. Equally important, Third World governments have also learned how to use their leverage in large procurements to realize additional gains through countertrade. Now that the methods, benefits, and risks of modern barter are better understood, it is likely that the use of countertrade as an alternative strategy for international business development will continue to grow.

THE ROLE OF THE SPECIALIST

Using countertrade does not require that a company develop new management structures, captive trading companies, or even additional overheads. Certain kinds and sizes of countertrade obligations and barter deals can perhaps best be handled by an in-house unit (e.g., the large offset obligations that Duke Golden described in chapter 7 as occurring at Northrop and the counterpurchase obligations that Jacques Rostain described in chapter 6 as evident at Combustion Engineering). However, it is important to remember that such units are generally expense centers, not profit centers. Stephen Crain described in chapter 8 the downfall of one such unit, which was converted to a profit center.

An exporter can contract with a specialist to handle the majority of its countertrade opportunities and should prepare itself to do so. If a company decides for at least part, if not all, of its countertrade to use the services of a third party for assistance, there have been traditionally three alternatives. The first is the specialized unit within the corporation—such as those that were discussed in chapters 6, 7, and 8. The second way to perform the countertrade is to go to a broker, a consultant, or a bank for information on how to structure the transaction and to whom to go to buy the products that may be offered in the countertrade in return for the supply contract; James Barkas (chapter 9) and Richard Cooper (chapter 11) discuss the roles of the banker and the consulting firm, respectively. The third source of assistance is the trading companies that can purchase products that are being offered to you by your customers as a condition of your sale to them.

Among the trading companies, there are those that have established a further specialization; the ones I call "specialized countertrading companies." They put together countertrade transactions for their clients and use the leverage of a trading company with which they may be associated actually to move the products economically for their clients.

What characterizes the specialized trading company are two things: first, it works on behalf of its client, which is generally most commonly the supply contractor to a country demanding countertrade. Its primary interest is to get the supply contract closed by using countertrade, rather than to find a better price on the commodity that may be involved in the countertrade. To that extent, the specialized trading company works as a subcontractor to the supply contractor, providing a service that helps it to close the deal.

The second defining feature of a specialized countertrading company is that it is often and most commonly a principal in the countertrade agreement between the supply contractor and the government involved. The countertrade company is most comfortable and in fact has the best chance to use its leverage on behalf of its client effectively, when it is actually negotiating a countertrade deal on behalf of the supply contractor. The countertrade company can generally not be as successful when it has no role in the negotiations but is instead basically a basket into which the products that are delivered to the supply contractor are deposited for disposition. In that kind of a situation a trading company might very well take products that a supply contractor has received and dispose of them but may have to dispose of them at liquidator's prices, which the supply contractor would have to absorb in the cost of its supply contract.

However, a countertrade specialist cannot do everything necessary to help the supply contract to be closed. First, the product has to be marketed and sold by the supplier, at least to the point where international payment becomes a problem.

Second, the buyer of the supplier's product has to have credit or at least has to be able to buy the product in local currency. Countertrade does not solve the problem of a buyer that cannot afford your equipment; it will not make the customer any more creditworthy. The buyer has to have bank credit, or money in the bank locally, since the countertrade generally generates income for another party within that country. All that the countertrade does for your transaction is to generate foreign exchange. That foreign exchange will be controlled by the central bank and does not help to pay back a local bank as far as local currencies are concerned. Those are two key distinctions.

The last one is important because it often is a source of confusion, and certainly a source of frustration, in countertrade. Salesmen will come back with a deal that they believed will be sewn up because a countertrade appears to be possible, and it turns out that the government agency does not have the budget for the purchase involved, or the private purchaser is in hock "up to his ears" and cannot even get local bank credit.

In a situation, however, where that local bank credit or the money in the government's budget exists, the specialized countertrader, such as MG Services, can do three things. First, it can structure, establish documentation for, and negotiate the countertrade program. Second, it can fulfill the obligation by executing the purchase contracts, in other words, buy for its own account and take title to the products. Also, it can arrange convertible currency financing.

At MG Services we formed a joint venture with First Boston Corporation, a major investment bank. Together we are offering to structure nonrecourse financing that is tied to trade transactions that will provide security for the repayment of those nonrecourse financing packages. It is a move away from the international project finance that has been common, particularly in the mining and petroleum industries, to other kinds of transactions and projects that are not self-liquidating as far as foreign exchange is concerned. The products that come out of the projects do not get sold in foreign markets and therefore do not generate foreign exchange. However, if the project or the equipment procurement of the government involved is of sufficiently high priority, that government may dedicate a portion of its output of an unrelated commodity or product that can be marketed internationally and dedicate the proceeds from the sale of those products to providing security for the financing.

To distinguish between the capabilities of specialized countertrading companies and to decide which one may be the proper company to use for any specific transaction, there are three basic distinguishing characteristics. First, what is the size of the transactions they are willing and able to underwrite? A $100,000,000 transaction is not something that a small trading company with $10 million worth of volume is in the best position to satisfy.

Second, what is the scope of products that they are capable of handling? The broader the variety of products, the less apt a company is to fall into the situation that Thomas McVey described in chapter 10 in which the bottom drops out of the market and leaves the company with no recourse to improve the terms of the sale. If a company has the alternative to shift to other products or has the alternative to take those products to a number of different markets, that flexibility can yield better terms for the entire transaction. A countertrading specialist that can deal in a variety of products not only in terms of different kinds of commodities but also different levels of value added certainly has more to bring to the transaction than otherwise.

Finally, and most importantly, countertrading companies differ in the number of countries in which they are currently purchasing and where they have the appropriate contacts and experience. The countertrade problem is not really what to do with the commodity that may be offered but how to make the transaction possible in a specific country. It is a common question we get from our clients. The first question they want to ask us is, "Can you handle copper rods from the Philippines?" That is not really the question that has to be answered before we determine whether or not a transaction can be done on a countertrade basis. Before one starts to focus on what products are available, and certainly one would have tried to insert the flexibility to deal in many more than just one product, more has to be known about the credit questions that we described earlier and how far along the contract negotiations have progressed.

GOVERNMENT-MANDATED COUNTERTRADE IN INDONESIA

It is useful to diagram a transaction to make it clear what kind of document flows we are talking about, what the complexities are, and how countertrade transactions these days are becoming more and more complex. One of the simplest of the transactions that is commonly being done is Indonesian counterpurchase. Over two years ago Indonesia introduced a requirement that government contracts of more than half a million dollars must involve a counterpurchase obligation by the foreign exporter. The exceptions involve companies that are sole sources of the needed import or have government support as far as the financing terms that they can offer. Most international competitively bid government contracts outside the military sector in Indonesia valued at more than half a million dollars have had the counterpurchase requirement imposed. This has been business that specialists have been able to do on behalf of the supply contractors.

The counterpurchase has two parallel transactions. The supply contractor sells its product to an Indonesian government agency and is paid for that product by means of a bank credit, an export agency credit, or perhaps even a letter of credit. Therefore, the exporter eventually gets its dollars from the government of Indonesia as a result of that financing. This is a straightforward sale for cash or bank financing except for one thing—that is, the exporter's parallel commitment to buy back from an Indonesian supplier.

These commitments, however, can be laid off to a third party. MG Services is one such third party, which is authorized by the Indonesian government to take assignment for that commitment. We sign an agreement with the supply contractor under which we take full responsibility for complying with his obligation to purchase from an Indonesian supplier a product and pay for it on normal commercial terms. The penalty is the liability to pay back to Indonesia 50 percent of the value of any shortfall in the purchase of Indonesian product. We get a fee from the supply contractor for assuming that obligation for him. We also provide to the government of Indonesia documents that prove the obligation has been fulfilled.

That is a very simple schematic of how Indonesian countertrade works. However, more and more today this type of transaction gets complicated. Additionality is also an important issue: governments require that the products that go out of the country be nontraditional exports, or if traditional exports, they must go to countries that have never bought before or have not been recent customers. In most cases, these countries have not bought for a simple reason: they do not have the foreign exchange to buy. Therefore, another barter is going to have to be arranged for us to get credit for an export from that country. MG Services' obligation thus becomes more complicated.

OBJECTIVES OF A COUNTERTRADE STRATEGY

A countertrade strategy can be used in a variety of ways to improve international business results:

1. It can help generate foreign exchange to speed up payments or make them possible at all.

2. It can provide offsets that make a supplier's terms more attractive.

3. It can put a supplier in a preferred position with its prime contractor.

4. It can earn the supplier a return for fulfilling third-party countertrade obligations.

The capability to structure, negotiate, and execute barter, counterpurchase, and bilateral clearing programs in a number of countries at once greatly increases the power of any countertrade strategy. One of the most convincing arguments in favor of relying on a specialist for assistance in using countertrade is its ability to put together transactions that involve a three-way or more complex trade and payments arrangement. For example, the counterpurchase required for the issuance of a license to import equipment from country A to country B may be fulfilled by arranging a barter for a country B export to country C. Payment from the purchaser of country C's product in country D goes to the exporter in country B. Unless such a transaction is large enough or the market important enough to justify the full-time attention of an accomplished negotiator, complex structures such as these are best achieved by working closely with a countertrade specialist whose capability in each of these countries is already in place.

The lesson is that if a company is confronted with countertrade, it should not walk away from the deal. By using the services of a specialist, a manufacturer or engineering company may find a way to turn a countertrade requirement to advantage and to open new fields of opportunity for its international business.

15

Switch Traders

BARRY F. WESTFALL

In our company, we look at countertrade as a form of trade financing. Thomas McVey (chapter 10) makes a very good point: ''After you have heard the first 'it can't be done' from your friendly banker, don't just assume that you must turn to countertrade.'' Chances are that there are other nontraditional forms of trade financing available that are more predictable, more efficient, and much less costly than countertrade. Countertrade for the sake of countertrade does not make sense. There is no reason to do it unless you have to. It has become a tool or technique that is used today to finance trade. It is one of the approaches that we take within ContiTrade Services.

CLEARING AND SWITCH TRADING

Clearing and switch trading are among the countertrade techniques that we use at ContiTrade Services.

Background on Clearing

In the period following World War II, the Eastern Bloc (COMECON) countries, which were without any hard currency, got together and formed bilateral trade agreements; they would exchange products back and forth without having to use hard currency. These bilateral trade agreements are typically established between the central banks of countries. *Swing limits*, like credit lines, are established between the two countries. The idea is that the countries ship products back and forth with the two central banks keeping score.

Ideally, the trade stays in balance, but in practice it never does: one country always takes more from the other than it ships back. The bilateral balances are expressed in terms of *clearing dollars*, and clearing dollars equate to the U.S. dollar. One country usually owes clearing dollars to the other. They do not stay in balance.

More recently, the COMECON countries established these bilateral trade agreements with other countries, primarily in South America. There evolved over time a situation in which countries like Colombia, Ecuador, Brazil and Argentina all had bilateral trade agreements with individual countries within the COMECON. Just as within COMECON, an imbalance almost always exists in some direction. Clearing, or switch, transactions have become much more important today than during the 1970s because of the liquidity crisis in South America. Traditional barter or countertrade does not usually work in most South American countries because the hard currency of those countries is controlled by the central banks.

The fact that some of these South American countries have active bilateral trade agreements with the COMECON enables us to use those trade agreements to facilitate triangular or multiangular deals. We will obtain a product from a third country but fit it into the bilateral trade agreement between the two, taking advantage of an imbalance that exists within that bilateral trade agreement. This procedure can be clarified with a few examples.

The first example involves what is really a form of the International Trade Certificates that Paul Boliek described in chapter 13. Through transactions with the Central Bank of Brazil, we are able to generate the right to import licenses in Brazil. These import licenses can be used by any importers in Brazil. The way we are able to do this is to identify an imbalance that exists between Brazil and one of the COMECON countries as far as their clearing account or bilateral trade is concerned. For example, if Hungary has purchased $50 million of soybeans, cocoa, coffee, or something else from Brazil, but has shipped nothing back, Hungary owes Brazil 50 million in clearing dollars. The Central Bank of Brazil has a credit on its books for $50 million, but there may be nothing in Hungary that they choose to buy. ContiTrade might approach the Central Bank of Brazil and make an arrangement whereby we will give them $50 million in cash in exchange for a credit in our favor in the clearing account with Hungary.

The $50 million credit that has been paid to Hungary for our account entitles us to take $50 million of products from Hungary, paying with that clearing credit, rather than with hard cash. If we are willing to make such an arrangement with the Central Bank of Brazil, which obviously is very favorable to Brazil, we need to have something in exchange; they give us in exchange the import-license rights equal to $50 million. In other words, we have the right to sponsor importers to CACEX, which is the agency that controls the Brazilian import licenses. We have no control over whether or not they will approve the products that are going to come in; the choice of products is always subject to their approval, but we do have the right to the licenses. The dollars that we have paid into Brazil that triggered the clearing payment are the dollars that are used by the Brazilians when they get their licenses under this program and pay for import. Switching can thus be seen as a way to facilitate the countertrade arrangements that were created by the bilateral trade agreement between the two countries.

That is our version of International Trade Certificates (ITCs). Today, it is limited to Brazil in that particular situation, but it is not limited as far as where the products come from. A major consideration about this and the one that Paul Boliek (chapter 13) touched upon (i.e., the ITCs) is that payment from Brazil still is not guaranteed. For example, if a U.S. multinational wants to sell to Brazil but his buyer needs import licenses because his allotment has run out, we sponsor him for import licenses. He gets the licenses and then is allowed to import. He is now allowed to open a letter of credit in favor of the exporter in the United States, but it is still up to the exporter to find a bank somewhere that will confirm that credit. Otherwise, the exporter has Brazilian risk from a payment standpoint.

One deal that solves the problem of payment risk is what we call a "direct switch." It could also be called a "classic clearing" or "switch deal." We ship a product to Brazil with payment made by the Brazilians in clearing dollars to a third country. The example involves our parent, Continental Grain, and a situation last year when Brazil desperately needed to import feed corn for livestock. At that time, Argentina, which traditionally is their number one supplier, was short of corn because they had oversold and had very little inventory available. This created a serious problem for Brazil, because normally when Brazil buys from Argentina, it does not have to pay today with cash, since there is a bilateral agreement between Brazil and Argentina. Brazil announced tenders to the grain traders of the world saying that it needed to buy a half million tons of corn and found that very few of the grain traders were even interested in participating in the tender, because there were no banks around that had an appetite for Brazilian risk. Everyone was concerned about being paid. We knew that Brazil had a large clearing credit with East Germany. Brazil had shipped to them, but East Germany had not been able to sell much back to Brazil. We approached the Brazilians with the proposal that we might be able to arrange for them to import corn from somewhere other than Argentina and to use East German clearing rather than hard currency to pay. They were interested.

We then approached the East Germans to talk about what they would do for us if we were to effect a clearing payment in their favor from Brazil, what products they would make available for us to take from East Germany in order to liquidate the transaction. Once we had a commitment there, we were able to go back to the corn desk at our parent company, Continental Grain, and say, "Okay, participate in the tender, but specify that payment will be made in Brazilian-East German clearing." At the same time we undertook an irrevocable commitment to pay Continental Grain cash upon presentation of documents when the corn was shipped to Brazil. The net result was that an export of American corn was sold by Continental Grain to Brazil. The Brazilian importer, upon presentation of documents, remitted cruzieros to the Central Bank of Brazil. They in turn made a clearing payment to East Germany (which was nothing more than a telex and a bookkeeping entry for our account). We then paid Continental Grain for the corn. They were completely out of the picture, and we now had credits or purchasing power in East Germany allowing us to buy products from East Germany in exchange for that clearing and to sell those products somewhere else for cash.

These types of transactions are complex. They are time consuming. However, they can be very fruitful: note that U.S. exports increased, Brazil got its grain and used some of its unused clearing dollars, and no one absorbed additional Brazilian risk. These deals are not limited to food products, and we are not limited to working only with our parent. However, this type of arrangement typically involves a product that a country like Brazil desperately needs, because there are many approvals that have to be received to put the whole thing together.

Multinationals that choose to use clearing and switch techniques should work with a qualified partner who is, without question, prepared to take all of the financial risk. The idea is for the company to end up with a transaction that is like that of the good old days: it ships its product, presents its documents, and gets paid. Whatever happens after that from a financial standpoint, the company will not need to worry.

16

Barter Merchants

JEROME K. LEVY

The Mediators is probably the oldest and largest media-buying service and re-ciprocal trade company in the United States. We are now in our twentieth year. The company actually started out as a media-buying service. We do not man-ufacture anything. We also do not warehouse anything.

Originally, there was no thought of barter at the Mediators. The company built quite a business for itself by buying media in wholesale lots and selling smaller blocks to major clients. However, this led to situations in which some of these clients started to ask the company whether we could take some product in exchange for advertising. Once we began accepting barter, the barter division of the company grew rapidly. Today, we do more than $400 million a year in annual sales in the barter end of the business. We represent some of the most popular names in corporate America including Eastman Kodak, Timex, Schwinn, and Wilson Foods. It is interesting that we came to this situation by accident.

One of the bases for our success is that we "swim against the tide." The basic business focus of most major corporations in the United States is upon selling: everything is sales—the vice-president of sales, January sales, February sales, and Christmas sales. The focus of the Mediators is upon buying.

There are many companies that manufacture a product and find themselves in a temporary imbalance and then unable to then sell that product for its full price. If they can sell the product continually for a full margin of profit, there is no substitute for cash. Barter is useful when normal cash or credit sales are inad-equate—no one can ever seriously say that barter is better than cash.

If a company has $10 million worth of inventory, and for whatever reasons, it cannot sell it at $10 million, what are its options? What can it sell the inventory for? Perhaps the company would be happy to sell it for $9 million. However, if it has to sell it for thirty cents on the dollar, that alternative would be unsatisfactory. Also, a dumping of bargain-priced goods on the market may alienate their best customers and distributors who paid full price for their inventory.

An alternative to selling at a steep discount or simply keeping excessive inventory is to barter the merchandise to a barter merchant such as the Mediators. Actually, what you are doing is *buying* other goods and services with the selling price value ($10 million) instead of cash. The Mediators buys the $10 million of goods. We will pay $10 million—but not in cash. We use something like the International Trading Certificates (ITCs) that Paul Boliek discussed in chapter 13. We establish trade credits with the corporation; this will permit it to use $10 million instead of cash in the payment of $10 million worth of goods and services.

In effect, this approach to countertrade, as well as the use of ITCs, is a type of clearing-account barter that Christopher Korth mentioned in chapter 1: We buy the goods or services but with credits that the seller can use at his leisure. The other goods and services we provide are primarily media advertising, the same advertising that the company is now buying for cash. However, the credits can also be used to buy raw materials or many other goods and services. Just as customer demand led the Mediators into barter, customer demand has also caused us to broaden our scope well beyond advertising.

What we do through this service is to take the inventory that the company has looked at as a liability, the product that it has overproduced and could sell only at a steep discount, and restore it to its original value, $10 million. The company is thus able to use the "full value" as an asset—not a deep-discounted liability.

We got into the barter business as a service for companies with excess inventory. However, we later carried the logic a step further. Many companies, even those without excess inventory, are not using all of their productive capabilities. They might only be manufacturing at 70 percent capacity, because they do not want to get stuck with 30 percent of excess product. What The Mediators will do is to buy part of the unused capacity. We will pay them the asking price for that, as though it were a finished product. From the manufacturer's perspective, this can be very profitable. Greater economies of scale can be realized. Also, there are no promotion costs, bad debts or collection costs. The profit on that 30 percent can be greater than the profit that the company is realizing on the other 70 percent of production. We are going to pay them the same price for that other 30 percent; they do not have any of those costs to bear; and, they have a higher profit. The only cost they may have on the 30 percent is the cost of raw materials and labor, since most indirect costs will typically have been fully amortized over the first 70 percent of production.

One of Mediators clients had excess salmon. The Mediators bought the entire position of salmon, had the client's cannery use its excess production time to can the salmon, took delivery in privately labeled salmon, and paid the client in advertising time based on the full value of canned salmon as though it were the client's famous brand name. This was followed by disposition of the private label salmon through retail channels of distribution that were noncompetitive to the original client's brand.

When the Jamaican government wanted to attract more U.S. tourists and introduce Jamaican-made product here they knew they lacked sufficient money for an effective advertising, marketing, and distribution campaign. Mediators stepped in and bought Jamaican rum in exchange for advertising, resulting in a successful campaign for Jamaica without them having to spend the cash.

These examples are but two of literally hundreds of major corporate trades in which the Mediators has participated as principal, ranging in size from small $1 million to $5 million amounts to as high as $100 million for a single contract.

Whether you call this unique process "barter," "reciprocal trade," "countertrade," or something else, the success record enjoyed by the Mediators in its relationship with hundreds of Fortune companies is clearly borne out by the satisfaction of the client corporations at the end of each contractual period and the many continuing ongoing contracts with the same companies year after year.

As long as American corporations continue to manufacture, sell, and compete for customers, and as long as "Mediators-style" barter can successfully satisfy corporate America's need for "full profit margins" and the ability to conserve cash by paying for goods and services with the "alternate capital" of excess inventory, barter and countertrade will flourish. The facet of barter that gives me the most pleasure, financial reward excepted, is the constant opportunity to be innovative, creative, and seeing it all come successfully together.

PART VI

TAX AND ACCOUNTING ASPECTS OF COUNTERTRADE

17

Accounting Aspects of Countertrade

ROBERT HENREY

The application of accounting concepts to exchanges of property raises numerous questions and uncertainties. Two issues recur that invariably involve an exercise of judgment: first, the timing of the recognition of any gain or loss on a given transaction and, second, the valuation of the property given up or received in the exchange. Although these brief remarks are directed to exchanges of property of a type that would normally be held for sale to others (i.e., inventory), many of the principles are applicable to exchanges involving services.

ACCOUNTING FOR INVENTORY VALUATION

Accounting literature as it applies to inventory valuation is well developed. The subject is of major importance in any attempt to measure the profitability of a given period in any situation in which the business acquires or adds value to property that will be sold within another period. Inventory-valuation concepts are the background against which all countertrade or barter transactions must be considered. Although accountants historically have had to deal with certain property transactions such as those involved in transfers between owners of a business and the business itself (capital contributions, dividends in kind, and so on) and the swapping of operating-type assets such as mineral leases and real estate, it was not until 1973 that an attempt was made to develop guidelines applicable to exchanges of assets includible in inventory.

Deferral of Gain from a Barter Exchange

The guidelines applicable to exchanges of assets includible in inventory were published as an opinion of the Accounting Principles Board (APB No. 29, May

1973: *Accounting for Non-monetary Transactions*). The key issue with which the opinion deals is whether or not gain recognition should always be deferred to the point at which cash (or more precisely a monetary asset or liability) enters the transaction cycle. To put it another way, if a business is successful in trading one type of inventory for another, does accounting caution and conservatism dictate that the carrying (or book value) of the inventory automatically carry over until such time as a "conventional" sale is made for cash or for a monetary receivable. The opinion comes down on the side of recognizing that an exchange of property should, at least in theory, be measurable and that its economic impact can be reflected in financial statements even if conversion into monetary assets and liabilities had not yet occurred. Thus as a general rule a transaction involving the transfer of property (passage of title) to another in exchange for other property may, under appropriate circumstances, be treated as an income- (or loss-) producing sale.

However, the opinion makes it clear that this general principle does not apply when inventory is swapped with similar inventory owned by another supplier merely to facilitate ultimate sale to customers. Such a swap would fail the recognition test since it would not be the "culmination of earnings process."

Valuation of Item Received by Barter

Having established the principle that income recognition on an exchange is to be the general rule, the major remaining issue becomes one of measurement: "Thus, the cost of a non-monetary asset acquired in exchange for another non-monetary asset is the fair value of the asset surrendered to obtain it, and a gain or loss should be recognized on the exchange" (APB 29, Paragraph 18).

What of the value of the asset received? The asset received is obviously included in inventory and will be subject to the regular and stringent inventory valuation rules. However, before even reaching that point, APB No. 29 qualifies its general rule by stating that the value of the asset received should be used if "it is more clearly evident than the fair value of the asset surrendered."

The issue of fair value may in practice severely limit the principle of income recognition. First, APB No. 29 itself includes a major qualification:

If neither the fair value of a non-monetary asset transferred nor the fair value of a non-monetary asset received in exchange is determinable within reasonable limits, the recorded amount of the non-monetary asset transferred from the enterprise may be the only available measure of the transaction. (APB 29, Paragraph 26)

Thus difficulties in fair-value determination may result in a mere carrying over of the book value of the sold inventory to the acquired inventory.

What guidance do we have as to what constitutes fair value of a nonmonetary asset? The opinion addresses the issue in general terms only: estimation of realizable values in comparable cash transactions, quoted market prices, independent appraisals, and so on. It is clear that in most cases the determination of fair value requires a careful study of all relevant factors affecting the marketability of the product. It is a study that will often involve the assessment of economic factors.

That assessment bears a surprising similarity to the kind of analysis that is required where product is being transferred between related parties in transactions that have a significant impact on the tax liability of both buyer and seller. In this case, the analysis is important not only from an accounting and tax point of view but also because it should be used to bring some objectivity to the economic desirability of a proposed countertrade transaction.

Experience indicates that a successful analysis requires a methodical review of all of the economic factors involved. As in an intercompany-pricing analysis, a thorough understanding of which elements contribute to value is essential. Some of these elements would be product and manufacturing intangibles, reliance on marketing intangibles, assumption of inventory risk, distribution costs, and present-value concepts.

It is possible that a fair value can be placed on a countertrade transaction that results in the recognition of a sale (which contributes to the enterprise's gross profit margin) and yet be faced with an inventory valuation problem with respect to the property received in exchange. The fair value placed on the trade becomes the cost of the property received. The new inventory item will now be subjected to the test that it be carried at the lower of cost or market. "Market" is not necessarily fair value. Essentially, "market" is defined in terms of current replacement cost (APB No. 43, Ch. 4, Paragraph 9). The emphasis has now shifted from the fair value of what was given up to the replacement cost of what was received.

The concept of replacement cost in the classic accounting literature is qualified by the principle that the market cannot exceed the net realizable value of the property, that is, the current estimate of the selling price reduced by costs of disposal. This evaluation process is continuous as long as the acquired property remains in inventory. The fair value on which the original countertrade was based is only relevant in terms of fixing historic cost.

Complex Transactions

The principles described in this brief review are relatively simple and broad in their application. In reality, countertrade transactions are often complicated by financing arrangements, "offset" contractual obligations, and the presence of more than two parties. A seller might, for example, receive cash for the transferred inventory but assume the obligation to purchase for cash from the seller agreed-upon quantities of an unrelated product at an agreed upon price over a given period; that would be a counterpurchase agreement. This obligation to take back the product would generally result in the retransfer of cash and in the assumption of complex performance obligations. While introducing contingencies (which would need to be evaluated from an accounting point of view under the concepts developed in the Financial Accounting Principles Board, Statement No. 5) into the overall picture, this type of transaction would still have to be analyzed by applying "recognition," "fair value," and "lower of cost or market" principles.

TAXATION OF COUNTERTRADE

The tax aspects of countertrade transactions are another area that can affect the cash flow and, therefore, the economics of a deal. In a case decided by the Supreme Court in 1979, which involved the deductibility for tax purposes of an inventory write-down, the Court reiterated a principle that has, over the years, added immeasurably to the difficulty of determining the taxability of business income: "There is no presumption that an inventory practice conformable to 'generally accepted accounting principles' is valid for tax purposes" (*Thor Power Tool Co. v. Commissioner* (99 SCK 773, Affirming CA7)). Although there is considerable common ground, tax-accounting principles are in some respects different from the accounting principles already discussed.

Property exchanges are likely to result in taxable income or loss since the concept of a "like exchange" or carrying over of the cost basis from one type of property to another is not available for inventory. This places a great deal of stress on the need to document "fair" or "fair market" values.

... Inventory write-downs which are necessary from an accounting point of view may be disallowed for tax purposes.

... Reserves for anticipated losses on contractual and other obligations which are required under generally accepted accounting principles will not give rise to current tax deductions.

APB No. 29 acknowledges that accounting for property exchange transactions will often be complicated by book/tax differences and that they will generally be timing, as opposed to permanent, differences.

CONCLUSIONS

It is apparent that accounting for many countertrade transactions requires careful thought and analysis. There are numerous subjective elements. However, the need to determine fair values should invariably result in good accounting practice, which will force management to take a more objective look at the economics of transactions. If the countertrader has set up an internal control system that requires that analysis be done before major countertrade deals are consummated, accounting disciplines can be used to enhance the quality of decision making.

18

Countertrade as a Tax-Planning Device

A. PATRICK GILES

TAX DEFERRAL ON U.S. EXPORTS

Domestic International Sales Corporation

Until recently, American law provided a tax deferral for the exporting income of a domestic international sales corporation (DISC). A DISC was typically a domestic subsidiary of a U.S. company engaged in exporting property that had been produced in the United States. The amount of deferral was limited to 42.5 percent of the DISC's income that exceeded the average income of the DISC over a base period.

DISC deferral was available on a percentage of income allocated to the DISC under special transfer-pricing rules. Transfer pricing was based either on special rules or arm's-length pricing under Internal Revenue Code Section 482. Under the special rules, transfer prices were based on either 50 percent of combined taxable income of the DISC or 4 percent of gross receipts from the transaction. Under either test the DISC would also earn 10 percent of the export-promotion expenses. There were also various qualification rules.

The DISC tax deferral was found to be an export subsidy by a panel convened under the rules of the General Agreement on Tariffs and Trade (GATT). (Michael Czinkota discusses GATT in chapter 23.) In response to this pressure, the United States has changed its tax law in relation to export trade. A new law, the Deficits Reduction Act of 1984, permits the formation of a new type of foreign (non-U.S.) tax-deferral company—the foreign sales corporation.

Foreign Sales Corporation (FSC)

The new law exempts from tax a portion of the export income of the FSC if certain foreign-presence and economic-process tests are met. To qualify as an FSC, the corporation must be organized outside the U.S. customs area. If the FSC is organized in a foreign country, that country must be either (1) a party to an exchange-of-information agreement with the United States or (2) an Income-Tax treaty partner, if the Treasury certifies that the exchange-of-information program under the treaty is satisfactory. So far, the preferred choice of jurisdiction to incorporate the FSC seems to be the U.S. Virgin Islands.

FSC benefits are generally provided only if the management of the corporation takes place outside of the United States and if the economic processes with respect to each transaction take place outside of the U.S. The management of the FSC is considered as outside of the U.S. if all meetings of the board of directors and shareholders are outside the United States, the principal bank account is outside of the United States, and all dividends and certain expenses are paid out of this bank account.

The economic processes are treated as outside of the United States if the FSC (or its agent) participates outside of the United States in the solicitation, negotiation, or making of the contract and if the foreign direct costs of the transaction incurred by the FSC are equal to or exceed 50 percent of the total direct costs (or 85 percent of direct costs of two activities). The cost of five activities are considered: (1) advertising and sales promotion, (2) processing of customer orders and arranging for delivery, (3) transportation and shipping, (4) determination and transmittal of a final invoice or statement of account and the receipt of payment, and (5) the assumption of credit risk.

The FSC benefits are also available for the export income of a corporation that elects to be a "small FSC" (one with up to $5 million of export gross receipts). A small FSC must be a foreign corporation that meets the requirements to be an FSC; however, a small FSC is *not* required to satisfy the foreign-presence and economic-process tests.

A portion of the FSC income that is considered to be foreign trade income (FTI) is exempt from U.S. income tax. FTI is FSC's gross income attributable to foreign-trading gross receipts, including profits from exports, commissions on exports of others, leases, and engineering and architectural services. The portion of FTI treated as exempt, which can be either 32 percent or approximately 70 percent, depends on special pricing rules used to determine FTI. Also, export income of an FSC will not be subject to the IRS rules relating to controlled foreign corporations (CFCs). However, the foreign sales corporation may not claim benefits under an income-tax treaty between the United States and a foreign country.

Nonexempt FTI generally will be treated as income effectively connected with a domestic U.S. trade or business and derived from U.S. sources.

COUNTERTRADE VIA AN FSC

Tax planners are always looking for ways to get a current deduction for expenses or loss and to defer taxes on profit. Because countertrade usually has a loss or expense on the purchase (or import) side and a gain on the sale (or export) side of the transaction, the classic opportunity for tax planning exists. The objective is to maximize the profit on the export side by using an FSC and to obtain a current deduction on the import side by using a domestic subsidiary to undertake and complete the counterpurchase obligation. Thus the new law has permitted U.S. exporters to defer indefinitely some of the profits on U.S. exports of goods and services.

Perhaps a hypothetical example would illustrate this point. For example, Company X is an exporter selling high-value computers and related software to Indonesia. The contract is in two parts, $10 million for the supply of the computers and software (on which the pretax profit is estimated at 30 percent or $3 million) and a $1 million six-month technical-assistance agreement (TAA) to install and test the equipment (pretax profit on this phase is estimated at 50 percent or $500,000). Company X has agreed to a counterpurchase of Indonesian rubber in the amount of $10 million and has assigned this liability to a commodity house and agreed to pay the commodity house a commission (or "disagio") of 10 percent or $1 million.

As can be seen in Exhibit 18.1, Company X would have a net profit of $1,650,000 if it carried out the transaction with its normal domestic sales subsidiary. However, the company could increase its after-tax profit on the transaction by approximately 23 percent by restructuring the transaction.

The company could use an FSC to supply the computers, software and engineering services. To simplify the example, it has been assumed that pricing would be on an arm's-length basis; the FSC guidelines permit 32 percent of such income to be tax deferred. (In an actual situation each company would have to examine with its accountants the most favorable FSC pricing rules.) Company X, through a domestic subsidiary, would enter into the counterpurchase obligation with Indonesia and assign the rubber to the commodity house, and the U.S. domestic subsidiary would pay the commodity house the commission of $1 million, which would be deductible against U.S. taxes (see Exhibit 18.2).

Nonexempt FTI is treated as income effectively connected with a domestic U.S. trade or business and derived from U.S. sources. If we assume that the domestic subsidiary, operating as the purchasing company and paying the $1,000,000 commission to the commodity house, owns the FSC, the nonexempt FTI, which in our example is $2,380,000, would be part of that subsidiary's gross income. The domestic subsidiary would deduct the commission paid (or loss on the import side) against its gross income and pay U.S. taxes on the remainder. The increase of $380,800 in after-tax profit is a direct result of the reduction of U.S. tax from $850,000 to $469,200.

The U.S. domestic subsidiary does not have to sell the counterpurchase products (in our example the Indonesian rubber) or pay the commission in the United States. It is only necessary that the domestic subsidiary undertakes the legal obligation to purchase the products or pay the commission. Where it discharges its obligation is irrelevant.

EXHIBIT 18.1

COMPANY X: A DOMESTIC EXPORT

Computer sale	10,000,000	
Pre-tax profit		3,000,000
Technical assistance agreement(TAA)	1,000,000	
Pre-tax profit		500,000
Total pre-tax profit (before commissions)		$3,500,000
Commission on sale of Indonesian rubber		(1,000,000)
U.S. pre-tax profit		2,500,000
U.S. corporate income tax (34%)		(850,000)
U.S. after-tax profit		$1,650,000
Exempt cash flow		0
After-tax profit and cash flow		$1,650,000

It has been reported that U.S. Customs is examining barter to determine whether imported products are being properly valued and reported for customs purposes. Many commentators have argued that barter transactions should be restructured as a counterpurchase to reduce the U.S. Customs risk of the transaction. Tax planning can now be added as another reason to restructure a barter into a counterpurchase.

The Internal Revenue Service

The problem with barter, from a tax-planning standpoint is that the loss on the purchase (import) side is netted against the gain on the sale (export) side. As stated above, the tax-planning objective should be to earn the gain on the export side in an FSC, where part of the gain can be tax deferred, and incur the

EXHIBIT 18.2

COMPANY X: EXPORT THROUGH AN FSC

FSC computer sale	10,000,000	
Pre-tax profit		3,000,000
TAA	1,000,000	
Pre-tax profit		500,000
FSC pre-tax profit (Assume that this amount is all FTI for FSC purposes)		$3,500,000
FTI (32%--assuming arms-length pricing)		(1,120,000)
Non-exempt FTI (treated as domestic subsidiary income & subject ot U.S. taxes)		2,380,000
Less: Commission on sale of Indonesian rubber		(1,000,000)
U.S. pre-tax profit		1,380,000
U.S. corporate income tax (34%)		(469,200)
U.S. after-tax profit		910,800
Exempt cash flow (FTI)		1,120,000
After-tax profit and cash flow		2,030,800

loss on the domestic side, where it can be currently deducted. This split of the gain and the loss forces the barter to be converted into a counterpurchase transaction.

If countertrade becomes more popular in the United States, the Internal Revenue Service (IRS) may examine countertrade and counterpurchase transactions with more care. The IRS's goal would likely be to allocate to the FTI of an FSC the expenses incurred to earn that FTI. Normally, those expenses would be ones that were incurred in obtaining the sale of the exported product. But the IRS could argue that the commission on the purchase of the *imported* product could be allocated to the FTI earned on the *exported* product.

CONCLUSIONS

This chapter offers a suggestion for using a foreign sales corporation in conjunction with barter to maximize after-tax U.S. profits. Thus it is suggested that a U.S. countertrade organization must have at least two legal operating entities. The first, the FSC, is used to maximize the profit on the *export* of the organization's products. The second, the U.S. domestic subsidiary, is used to fulfill the counterpurchase or countertrade obligation and thus maximize the loss, if any, on completing that obligation. The income would be maximized in the low-tax subsidiary (i.e., the FSC) while the expenses were concentrated (legally) in the high-tax domestic subsidiary.

19

A View from the IRS

FRED T. GOLDBERG, JR.

There is no literature and no institutional knowledge on the subject of the tax aspects of countertrade. This is clearly a significant form of commercial activity that has tax consequences associated with it. However, countertrade does not fit neatly into any of our preestablished boxes. We have a tax system that operates with certain assumptions about how the commercial world operates. Barter is only one example of how the commercial world is engaging in business enterprises that do not fit within the compartments we have established. Foreign currency is another illustration. The taxation of foreign-currency transactions is a mess; we just have not figured out how to deal with it in terms of the tax system.

Another ambiguous area is property interest. Traditionally, you own it, sell it, buy it, or maybe lease it, generally for cash or deferred payment in cash. The whole tax system is structured around those kinds of notions.

However, the world is rapidly bypassing this system with things like futures, options, options on futures, and futures on options. The market is segmenting ownership interests by time, and the tax code has a great deal of trouble dealing with those types of arrangements. People are also carving up property interests in ways such as multiple-class trusts and other arrangements that stratify ownership interest in different pieces of principal, different pieces of an income stream. Again, the tax system is not structured to deal with those types of arrangements.

To some extent, countertrade poses some analogous concerns. There are many potential tax pitfalls to countertrade. People are entering into very plausible, very reasonable, and very appropriate commercial arrangements for which there may be unforeseen tax consequences waiting in the wings. Conversely, there are opportunities in a countertrade context for tax-planning activities that will minimize the tax liability of one or both parties.

From a tax perspective, we perceive three basic forms of barter. The first involves a simple swap by a U.S. tax-paying company of a product that it manufactures directly in exchange for a product that another company manufactures; thereafter, the taxpayer either disposes of or uses that second product. The second form is a counterpurchase arrangement where a U.S. taxpayer sells nominally for cash or deferred payments and through a protocol separately contracts for the purchase of products from the other party or from others acceptable to that party. The third arrangement is a "compensation" or "buy-back" arrangement whereby the U.S. taxpayer in effect sells a production facility and agrees to take back the output from that facility in compensation for or in consideration for constructing the facility in the first place.

When tax aspects are considered, there are three critical questions: How much? When? Where? For tax purposes, the answer to "How much?" is that you naturally want your gross income as low as possible and your deductions as high as possible. In terms of "when," you want your deductions now and your income later. "Where" depends upon your foreign-tax-credit situation and sourcing rules. The Internal Revenue Service perspective is that we just want to tax you on what is fair and at the right time.

As a starting point, the export leg and the cross-purchase activity each arise in the customary and/or perhaps customarily arcane and murky world of international tax planning. For example, you have treaty considerations. Given the structure of your international tax situation, from where do you want to run the selling leg of the transaction? Is it to be through a U.S. domestic subsidiary? Is it a foreign subsidiary that is doing the sale? What are the roles of foreign subsidiaries in affecting pieces of the transaction from a tax-planning standpoint? You have foreign tax-credit considerations. If you are in an excess-credit position, where do you want to be putting your income? Where do you want to be putting your deductions? What kind of allocation issues arise? These questions come up whenever a company, a U.S. taxpayer, is selling abroad.

Under the new legislation, you have foreign sales corporations—do you want to run your export activity through a foreign sales corporation? Or do you want to use a possessions corporation for purposes of getting a possessions-corporation tax credit? All of these factors that enter into any international tax-planning endeavor play the comparable role in deciding "what am I going to do with respect to my export leg in a countertrade context?" You also have foreign-currency issues that virtually defy comprehension. If either leg of the transaction is occurring in a context that involves a foreign currency, you have to sort through all of the foreign-currency issues in structuring the deal as well.

With respect to "how much," if you have a straight barter transaction, the issue is very direct. How much is your income? You are shipping machines and you are getting commodities back. How do you value the two legs of the transaction? When is your income on the sale of those machines in exchange for the commodities coming back? When you get to counterpurchase, it gets a little more tricky because you have nominal pricing. For example, a company is selling machines for cash and then turning around and buying commodities for cash. Since cash is received, the "how much" question is simpler. In compensation transactions where there is a long-term undertaking to build a facility coupled with the taking of products out of that facility in exchange, you are depending on how the contract is structured. You may be dealing with a pure barter—a pure valuation question—"How much am I being compensated for building this facility?" If you have a nominal-pricing arrangement, you are dealing with a "how much" that at least nominally is fixed.

With respect to "how much," you have an issue that relates to components. In other words, it is not a simple matter of selling the machines, either in exchange for commodities or in exchange for cash, with something coming around the other end. You are selling equipment. You are also selling long-term services, training, technology. From a tax standpoint you need to answer "how much" with respect to *each* of those components because the tax treatment of each of those components may vary significantly.

The components question also comes up in the context of the International Trading Certificates (ITCs), which Paul Boliek discussed in chapter 13. When that system is employed in barter, the importer receives, along with the product, a certificate that gives him the right to export to the country from which he bought. That may be a valuable instrument; therefore, the importer is paying for two things: raw materials, and an export certificate that is a separate asset with basis associate and, when I subsequently dispose of that asset, I have income. If you wash through it all, assuming you are going to hold on to the export certificates for a while, from the revenue standpoint, the inclination would be not to allocate a separate piece of the price to it. That, in effect, would reduce your cost of raw materials, which would, in turn, have an effect on your income.

Again, with respect to the "how much" question, the most interesting aspect arises because of the commercial pressure to overstate the income on the export leg. In general, the tendency is for the country that is exporting the raw materials to inflate its nominal price on the exported raw materials. The U.S. manufacturer's response may well be to inflate its prices in return. That may or may not lead to higher taxes.

To the extent that you had a distortion in the nominal prices, it washes out: both the revenue and corresponding cost are overstated. The net effect is that the distortions do not really have a material effect—as long as the exchanges are simultaneous or at least in the same tax period.

The situation is more complicated with arrangements that involve much longer-term intercourse between the parties (e.g., many counterpurchase contracts). If machinery that is worth only $90 is sold today for $100, and I agree to buy $100 of products that in the future are also really worth only $90, it would appear that the taxpayer has front-loaded too much income: income comes early and the offsetting loss comes late (or vice versa). That would appear to create a distortion that is not correct from an economic standpoint. Therefore, it should also not be correct from a tax standpoint. However, you may be paying more tax dollars that you should. The question relates to when the income and cost are recognized. The general rule is to recognize when you ship or take delivery of the product, if you are an accrual basis taxpayer.

That example seems relatively straightforward. The only issue is whether you can argue for deferral of the income under the installment method. A dealer may find it hard to qualify for the installment rule. But if the dealer does qualify, the installment-sale provisions may give some way to defer recognition of the income for a delayed-barter exchange. There is an argument depending on how the transaction is structured that you can claim what we call "open transaction treatment." That is something that the IRS does not like very much. Generally, the courts do not like it either. Basically what it says is "you sold this but we do not know how much you sold it for because whatever it is you are getting, we cannot value it today." Therefore, you do not report any income until you get it. Again, it is an issue.

With respect to compensation or buy-back arrangements, there is, first, a very interesting threshold question. If I agree to build a plant abroad in exchange for production from that plant, is that a recognition transaction? Have I sold this facility? It is similar to selling the facility for cash. That threshold question poses a lot more ambiguities than are readily apparent. The IRS position would be that it may be a recognizing event: you have just had a taxable event and you have to pay on the income you get from building and selling the plant.

If that is the proper characterization, you get into what we call the "completed contract method of accounting." If it is a long-term contract to build a facility, the question is whether one can defer reporting the income from that transaction until one has completed its performance. The same thing would apply for long-term equipment manufacturing. The completed contract method of accounting lets you defer recognition of income until you are done, which is part of the object. For this last class of activity, there is no reason to structure it necessarily as a sale giving rise to taxable income. You can structure it as a joint venture. You can then move around the tax consequences and the tax benefits associated with the activity to benefit the taxable entity involved. It is something, particularly in the very sophisticated, large-scale projects that are taking place abroad, where someone should ask whether a sale has inadvertently been created when a joint venture would be better for tax purposes?

Something else to bear in mind is that in the 1984 Tax Act, Congress adopted a number of so-called "time value of money" provisions—the original issue discount (OID) rules, below market-loan provisions. All of these provisions were intended to recognize that in any deferred arrangement there is an interest component, even if it must be imputed interest. For example, Uncle Sam is now requiring you to charge 12 percent when you sell the family farm. The rules are extremely broad and, if you have a deferred-barter transaction or a compensation arrangement that is characterized for tax purposes as a sale, you have a deferred-payment element. Under the new law, that deferred-payment element is to be bifurcated into a principal piece and into an interest piece. But when you get outside of that very simple structure and you start talking about an international transaction involving what we would call "payments in kind" where valuation and time of performance are perhaps problematic at best, to try to superimpose these so-called "time-value rules" gets to be very very difficult. It is clear on the face of the statute that it will have an effect on these deferred arrangements. It is something that you at least need to get somebody sorting through to see if you are affecting yourself.

Now, it turns out that in a lot of these cases, it may be to the company's advantage. What it does is to let you discount the purchase price and then pick up the interest over time, if you are the seller. So it may turn out that it is a windfall to those of you who are exporting.

The final piece is "where?" Treaty considerations, foreign-tax-credit considerations, and other considerations have to factor into any decision on how to structure the mechanics of any international trading effort including, as a subset, countertrading on the export leg. There is a very interesting planning question here. We revenuers should be pleased since the companies overstated all of their income. We are going to tax you on your $100 gross income this year knowing that $10 of that is a little high, and then you are going to get your $10 deduction on the other end next year when you close the transaction.

A suggestion has been made to bifurcate the arrangement: The purchase side would be done through an FSC (Foreign Sales Corporation). The principle would also work analogously through a possessions corporation (e.g., through a Puerto Rican subsidiary). It will also work in a foreign-tax-credit situation if you need to move income somewhere for a certain reason or for treaty reasons. The basic point is that the extra income is taken in your FISC. The effect of doing that or the effect of dropping it into a low-tax jurisdiction or the effect of running it through a Puerto Rican activity is that there is a phoney $10 of income that either is not taxed or is taxed at a much lower rate. On the other side, the transaction is structured so that the commodities are bought nominally for $100 when both parties know full well that the goods are going to be dumped for $90—thus triggering a $10 loss. The goods may perhaps be purchased through a U.S. company so that $10 of phantom loss is generated domestically against U.S. income.

It is a variation on the time-honored theme of tax planning. That is what people are doing, but it is not clear that it works. It is highly likely to be subject to attack under section 482, which gives the commissioner very broad authority to reallocate items of income, expense, deduction, credit, and the like among related taxpayers.

I hope that these examples have illustrated the basic point, an obvious point perhaps with which I started. Countertrade is being driven by realities much larger and much more real than the Internal Revenue Code but that, nonetheless, need to be worked through that filter.

PART VII

OFFICIAL PERSPECTIVES TOWARD COUNTERTRADE

20

Countertrade: A View from the U.S. Congress

DON BONKER

INTERNATIONAL TRADE

International trade is an issue whose time has come in Congress. As much as environment was a major issue in Congress in the 1960s and energy was the dominant issue in the 1970s, in the late 1980s it is going to be trade. The importance of the trade issue in Congress can be seen by looking at the activities of various congressional committees and their efforts for expanding their respective jurisdictions so that they can take part in the trade action. Also, the young, aspiring, highly motivated staff assistants who come to the nation's Capitol seem to flock where the important issues are: right now that migration is toward trade activity.

Similarly, you can look at the newspapers where trade used to be a subject that was very seldom mentioned; now it is a dominant issue not only in the business section of the major newspapers but also in the headlines of the front page. Each month the secretary of commerce announces the trade deficit for the preceding month. The announcement makes front page news in the *Washington Post*. In past years, it was seldom even mentioned in the newspaper. Thus it would indeed seem that international trade is an issue whose time has come.

More and more the American people are beginning to realize how much trade affects our domestic economy. The simple fact is that our domestic economy is no longer sufficient to meet our gross needs. At the same time, we find ourselves in a fiercely competitive international economy. The United States needs to find its place not only globally but also in the domestic market. Recent statistics indicate that consumer demand in the United States is up significantly but that domestic production is down. Growth is continuing in this country, but it is not domestic growth. This growth is being met by imports, resulting in staggering trade deficits. Those trade deficits, which are going to get bigger before getting smaller, do have policy implications in Washington.

In Congress we regard this as a dilemma: there are two ways to reduce this trade deficit—either to export more or to import less as a result of protectionism. Despite the protectionist furor, there is strong preference for export promotion. But how do we facilitate export opportunities? How do we become more competitive in the world market? How can we market and distribute our products in a way that would get that export figure up?

Increased exports are difficult to achieve. So people look toward solutions to the import-related problem; that's why the protectionist impulse is very real and is growing in Congress.

INTERNATIONAL COUNTERTRADE

Countertrade is one of the trade areas of interest in Congress and in the administration. However, the attitude of the U.S. government is inconsistent. There is no overall policy.

The U.S. government generally views countertrade as contrary to an open, free-trading system. However, as a matter of policy, although the government does not sanction countertrade, it tolerates it and will not generally oppose U.S. companies participating in countertrade arrangements. Nevertheless, strong opposition would certainly arise if such arrangements could have a negative impact on our national security.

The U.S. government will provide advisory and market intelligence services to U.S. business, including information on the application of U.S. trade laws. The U.S. government will continue to review on a case-by-case basis financing for projects containing countertrade or barter—taking into account the distortions caused by these practices. The U.S. government will also participate in reviews of countertrade by international organizations such as the International Monetary Fund (IMF), the Organization for Economic Cooperation and Development (OECD), and the General Agreement on Tariffs and Trade (GATT). Finally, the U.S. government will exercise caution in the use of its own barter authority, reserving it for situations that present advantages not offered by conventional market operations.

The U.S. position regarding countertrade is admittedly contradictory. Officially, the U.S. opposes mandated countertrade, recognizing that it distorts trade: it *is* contrary to free trade, and it *is* inefficient—as several of the other authors in this book have indicated. Yet the $123 billion trade deficit compels the United States to engage in countertrade to preserve its market share, particularly in Third World countries and other countries that demand or require some form of countertrade. I think that Lionel Olmer had the best statement. He recently observed before one of the U.S. Congressional committees that an increasing number of countries have endorsed or encouraged countertrade arrangements and that the likelihood of the trend continuing is high. He further noted that, for some companies wishing to do business in developing countries, these arrangements appear to offer the only real hope of making a sale, for maintaining or expanding market share.

I do not think that there need by any fear of future legislative or executive branch actions either to inhibit countertrade activity or to limit U.S. participation in countertrade worldwide. It is also doubtful that the United States will pursue efforts through multilateral institutions to come to grips with this problem before it becomes institutionalized worldwide.

Offsets

Notwithstanding the U.S. government's official position against countertrade, it has been guilty in the past, as Christopher Korth indicated in chapter 1, of actually participating in or promoting countertrade. For example, the Defense Department not only has facilitated countertrade arrangements (such as the offsets in the sale of defense-related products that Duke Golden discussed in chapter 7) but also has provided, until recently, guarantees for some offset arrangements.

Offset occurs as a result of an agreement in which an American firm commits to make some investment in a foreign country in order to buy goods and services from that factory in the foreign country in exchange for foreign commitments to buy the U.S. firm's goods. This pertains mostly to defense-related items. Typically, foreign countries now demand that some portion of a defense-manufacturer's subcontract work be awarded to firms in that country or that the American company agree to some coproduction of its product in that foreign country. It has been estimated that during the next five years this kind of offset arrangement will amount to $6 billion a year.

Congress is concerned about these offset trends. At least one House committee has already had hearings. The General Accounting Office (GAO) has issued a report pointing out that foreign governments are putting pressure on U.S. companies for economic concessions and that this raises questions of whether we are shipping American technology and jobs overseas and what impact this is having on our industrial base. The rough estimate of jobs lost as a result of these offset arrangements has been 175,000 to 200,000 direct jobs lost. The GAO has recommended that Congress direct the administration to institute a policy to resist these offset demands by foreign governments, particularly when they involve U.S. foreign aid in terms of foreign military sales, credits, or grants to various countries. So Congress may act on this particular issue.

The Commodity Credit Corporation

Another example of government participation is the Commodity Credit Corporation (CCC) of the Department of Agriculture. The Department of Agriculture, through the CCC, between 1950 and 1973 actually engaged in almost $2 billion of barter of strategic materials obtained from other countries in exchange for U.S. agricultural products. This practice supposedly was suspended in 1973, but due to a stockpiling of agriculture products, the pressure is growing again for some kind of barter arrangements for strategic materials. Recently the United States worked out an agreement with Jamaica for bauxite in exchange for dried dairy milk. Thus the government, despite its official position, is again actually engaging in various forms of barter trade.

The Export Administration Act

The Export Administration ACT (EAA), which is pending in Congress, deals primarily with foreign-policy and national-security controls that inhibit our export opportunities. For many people in the business community, this is the biggest trade issue in Congress. However, in the section of the bill entitled ''Materials in Short Supply,'' there is an amendment that deals specifically with barter arrangements. In fact, the bill provides that the secretary of agriculture shall submit to Congress a report on the status of federal programs relating to the barter or exchange of commodities owned by the CCC for materials and products produced in foreign countries. Such a report shall include details of and changes that are necessary in existing law to allow the Department of Agriculture to implement fully any barter program. That is certainly contrary to our official position on mandated barter programs of other countries. Yet this provision is in the EAA—and my staff informs me that this same provision is in at least three other laws that are in effect today.

The EAA goes on to say that, notwithstanding any other provision of law, the president is authorized to barter stocks of agricultural commodities that have been acquired by the government. Such commodities can be exchanged for petroleum and petroleum products and for other materials vital to the national interest that have been produced abroad in situations in which the sales would not occur except via barter. Indeed, several objectives of the U.S. government are accomplished by such transactions. On the one hand, the Department of Agriculture is eager to get rid of all of these commodities that have been stock-piled over recent years. On the other hand, for national-security interests, it is a major imperative of our policy that we have access to strategic materials. Thus barter is consistent with both agricultural policy and national-security policy— despite the fact that it is contrary to the official position of this government on mandated countertrade.

The Export Trading Company Act

The recently passed Export Trading Company Act is intended to encourage and facilitate U.S. exports. Yet in all of the hearings that we conducted on this subject, there was little discussion about countertrade. Countertrade was not much of an issue in 1980–82. Yet inherent in that legislation is a new government policy that sanctions countertrade because the act permits export trading companies and bank holding companies to engage in various forms of countertrade. One U.S. government analyst said it this way, ''Once these banks and major businesses become accustomed to it, and once the supporting information and transaction systems become routine, large barter-trading networks may develop.'' One interpretation is that export trading companies will gradually lead countertrade down the road to respectability. That was not a conscious intention when the legislation was enacted, but that very well could be an effect.

MULTILATERAL INSTITUTIONS

The United States always prefers to go to the IMF, GATT, OECD, or some other multinational organization if it has complaints rather than to develop unilateral policies. We want to have the same ''level playing field'' for everyone. The United States, if it intends to do anything about countertrade, will pursue it through these various institutions.

The International Monetary Fund

The IMF firmly opposes mandated countertrade, much as the United States does. Yet, ironically, the austerity programs that the IMF imposes upon developing countries often cause these countries to resort to countertrade. Invariably, the austerity measures, which the IMF imposes upon many countries receiving its aid, call for importing less and exporting more. That can make it very difficult on U.S. exporters. In any case, these adjustment programs, which are intended to bring about austerity, seem to spawn more countertrade because countries have few other options if they want to import goods.

In 1983 the IMF clarified its position in one of its policy statements by stating: ''The Fund's policy on countertrade practices is to encourage its members to rely on appropriate fiscal, monetary and exchange-rate policies rather than on restrictive practices to achieve balance-of-payment adjustments.''

The World Bank

The World Bank has no formal policy regarding countertrade. It does not consider the presence or absence of a barter commitment when evaluating project financing in developing countries. In other words, when it engages in heavy loans, countertrade is not a factor that is considered. Neil Roger gives us a view from the World Bank in chapter 22.

The General Agreement on Tariff and Trade

GATT policies do not apply to private countertrade activities. However, if countries feel compelled, because of unfair trade practices, to bring a dispute to the organization, countertrade could well be one of the issues raised, although there is currently no identifiable clause that relates to countertrade within GATT. Michael Czinkota examines GATT's view in more detail in chapter 23. [Editor's note: A new GATT round began in August 1986.]

The Organization for Economic Cooperation and Development

The OECD is the industrialized nations' vehicle for dealing with these issues. It is on record against government-mandated countertrade. Thus when members such as the United States or France require countertrade, they are actually acting contrary to OECD policy.

Many international organizations have been, and will continue to be, looking at countertrade and formulating positions. If the agency is dominated by the industrialized countries, it is likely to be against countertrade—despite actions of individual member governments. If the international organization is dominated by Third World countries, it is going to be more supportive of countertrade.

SUMMARY AND CONCLUSIONS

Countertrade is emerging as a prominent issue in international trade. There are benefits that relate to market access. Many less developed countries actually have a liquidity crisis: they have debt problems, and the availability of foreign exchange is such that they cannot pay cash for the imports they want. If we are going to maintain any market access in these countries, countertrade is probably going to be a way of life. I do not see the credit situation improving in the short term. Countertrade does enable these countries to continue trading to obtain needed imports and to keep global trade flows moving.

I think that, as a policy, the U.S. government is going to tolerate countertrade. Also, countertrade can reduce pressure on the dollar. With the inflated dollar hurting our trade and indeed impacting our domestic economy, we need ways to reduce demand for the dollar. Countertrade does just that by reducing the need for dollars to finance international transactions.

But there are also problems, particularly for smaller and medium-sized companies. Larger corporations are generally more flexible and more familiar with international market flows. Small and medium-sized companies are more likely to have great difficulty if they encounter countertrade requirements in other countries. Japan has a tremendous advantage over the United States. Its 5,000 to 8,000 trading companies actually make a marketing opportunity available to its smaller industries. In the United States, without export trading companies, our smaller companies simply do not have an opportunity to engage in this kind of trade.

For Congress and the executive branch, the policy issues are apparent. Should we continue officially to oppose government-mandated countertrade? I think yes.

But we have to be consistent: we cannot, on the one hand, say that we oppose it and, on the other hand, indulge in the practice, which is exactly what we are doing today. The executive branch must sort this out.

The United States may consider accepting government-mandated countertrade with the poorest countries as a trade concession. We are sensitive, as a policy matter, to the poorest of the poor—countries that may be less inclined toward democracy if they are economically depressed. That is what usually invites revolution. We are seeing these problems in both Sudan and Peru today. They must be given an opportunity to flex their economic muscles. Maybe countertrade, restricted to these particular countries, can help them and also help our exporters as well.

Countertrade contracts should be protected from U.S. foreign-policy control. Some of these countertrade contracts are long term. We run into the problem, notably with Eastern Bloc countries and especially with the USSR, that their actions might provoke presidential decree to terminate contracts. This happened in the Carter years with the grain embargo. It happened again in the Reagan years on the pipeline with the invasion of Afghanistan. In the EAA there is a contract-sanctity provision that removes the president's authority to terminate existing contracts in the future. We do not want to see an abuse of presidential authority. We want to restore our credibility as a reliable supplier. However, it is not clear whether or not countertrade contracts would be exempt. This is something that should be considered by Congress.

Finally, we ought to take our case to the GATT so that it could develop some international guidelines with respect to countertrade. Although Congress has not dealt directly with countertrade in detail, it is an issue that is pending as we examine unfair trading practices. Overall, Congress will be responsible in how it deals with this issue. It has been with respect to import-related problems and with what is happening to our industrial base as a result of cheap imports. I have no reason to believe that Congress is going to do anything rash about countertrade. The least we can do is try to be consistent in our policies.

However, in terms of the global trade community, we are going to have to deal more precisely with the strength of the dollar, with the Third World debt crisis, with protectionism, and with unfair trade practices as they exist in other areas. But the big political question will be whether we have the willpower to sometimes go against our best interests in order to set a higher standard. By officially proclaiming that countertrade, subsidies, and other unfair trade practices are not the right way to go, the United States can set that standard and follow it itself. We will have a better global community, and it most certainly will enhance our own domestic economy.

21

Countertrade: A View from the U.S. Department of Commerce

FREDERICK E. HOWELL

RECENT DEVELOPMENTS IN INTERNATIONAL COUNTERTRADE

No matter where you look today, countertrade is increasingly becoming a major factor in international trade. The range of products involved in countertrade is very broad: aerospace, energy, agriculture, construction, telecommunications, consumer products, and so on.

U.S. companies are joining in the process of countertrade more than in the past. This increased involvement in countertrade has typically been as a result of requirements of foreign governments or a countering of the countertrade offers of our competitors. But increasingly, our companies have become more aggressive in the use of countertrade. Our companies are beginning to participate and initiate more effectively rather than merely respond to these transactions.

DEFINITION

An examination of countertrade is very often limited to trade (e.g., barter, counterpurchase, buy-back, bilateral clearing agreements, switch and swap trading). However, more and more international barter includes an investment element: coproduction, joint ventures, industrial cooperation, investment-performance requirements, local content, and low or nonequity investment. These terms are not traditionally considered part of what more narrowly might be construed or defined as countertrade. But they are part of the family—a part that is also growing.

In addition, the lines between military and nonmilitary trade are less clear.

Offsets have traditionally been considered as military. But this also is changing. "Military" offsets are partially nonmilitary more often than not—and increasingly so. Although one leg of the transaction may be military (e.g., military vehicles or aircraft), the other leg—the offset requirement—may not be military.

THE U.S. GOVERNMENT'S PERSPECTIVE

Whether or not the U.S. government views the growth of countertrade in a positive or negative light, it is obvious that the U.S. government must have a policy with regard to countertrade. So far, the U.S. government (the executive branch, at least) has kept a fairly even "hands-off" policy regarding barter. It expects the private sector to respond effectively to the need to educate itself and help itself through the export trading companies, through the consultant firms, or through banding together and essentially doing what is needed to compete effectively in world markets.

Opposition to Countertrade

In general, the U.S. government opposes countertrade as both uneconomical and trade distorting. The government is particularly opposed to government-mandated countertrade. It is this use of leverage in the market that most concerns the government with respect to countertrade in all of its manifestations. The government is prepared to attempt to limit the use of countertrade by making representations to foreign governments and by participating in multilateral trade fora. Institutions such as the Organization for Economic Cooperation and Development (OECD) and the United Nations can try to understand better what the countertrade process is and how it is impacting on our trading system. They also should try to develop a consensus on how to deal with such trade. Is it distorting the trading system? Is it helping the trading system? Is it trade creative, or is it trade restrictive? If it is both, in what specific ways can we measure the impact?

Toleration of Countertrade

Despite the U.S. government's basic opposition to countertrade, its policy is not designed to intervene against U.S. companies participating in countertrade per se. Its policy is not to pursue a company for having participated in countertrade or for contemplating countertrade. The thought is more that U.S. companies engage in these practices at their own risk and based on their own best judgment of what the problems might be.

The government will help with traditional trade-information services. It will provide basic market intelligence. It will not promote countertrade but will give the same type of market intelligence that is given in other areas. So countertrade is not discriminated against in that sense by the government.

Initially, when countertrade came to the forefront, there were those who thought that there were ways for countertrade to circumvent U.S. import laws. Policy is not designed to allow that. The existing laws will apply fully to countertrade in all of its forms: whether there is dumping being exercised through the use of countertrade, whether there is subsidization involved, or whether there is an unfair trade practice of some kind involved, U.S. trade law will apply.

There have been some problems with U.S. Customs. Customs has some difficulty with valuation and determination of the transaction value of countertraded goods and services. But it is learning to cope with the problem of countertrade. Although it does not specifically ask the U.S. trader to identify whether or not an imported good is coming in as a result of countertrade, it does prefer to know. It is in your best interest to be as forthcoming as possible in providing that information for Customs. Eventually, U.S. Customs might specifically ask the U.S. importer if the goods coming into the U.S. are as a result of a countertrade arrangement.

These are the basic points of the U.S. government's policy on countertrade. I will now expand a little on each one of the points.

Countertrade Is Seen to Be Trade Distorting

The U.S. government sees countertrade as "trade distorting" because it tends to involve government more in commerce and because it tends to politicize international trade. If governments do not directly mandate the practice, they often create the conditions that compel private-sector entities to countertrade. They may not be directly mandating the countertrade, as in the case of Indonesia or Colombia, but they may set up the exchange controls or import-licensing programs or other constraints that cause the trading community to resort to countertrade. The sellers are forced to become buyers. Countertrade is often managed in such a way as to reinforce industrial policy and export targeting of the importing country.

One of the major problems is that countries are increasingly using countertrade to promote their industrial development. What results is not simply a trade transaction but forced participation in what the government of the country requiring this reciprocity sees as its own best interests in developing its industries or its exports. By telling which products you can countertrade and under what conditions you can countertrade, they structure their import and export flows in a way that is, in our view, trade distorting.

We see it somewhat as "beggar-thy-neighbor." We would prefer that the governments remove themselves a step from this process and let the market determine the flow of goods. We see countertrade as a derogation from "most-favored nation treatment." Very often terms of discrimination occur merely by virtue of implementation of countertrade. There is some implicit discrimination in that some companies are not as well equipped as others to deal with it. They may never be, unless they band together with other companies, because they do not have the export resources typically needed in countertrade or the capacity to absorb the products that they would have to take back in countertrade.

MULTILATERAL CONSIDERATIONS

Violation of the nondiscrimination policy in most-favored nations is a danger with regard to the General Agreement on Tariffs and Trade (GATT). With all of its failings, GATT is still the best thing we have in international trade discipline. Our concern is that the GATT will become even further weakened as countries begin to incorporate these reciprocity clauses into their trade programs. Michael Czinkota addresses this issue of the GATT perspective in chapter 23.

Partially at the initiative of the United States, the Organization for Economic Cooperation Development (OECD) developed a paper on countertrade, which is available to the public. The OECD study gives us a clear idea of where there may be trade distortions in the practice, and it also gives us a better information base from which to draw.

In spite of the effort at the OECD to study the issue, there has been as yet no consensus even among industrialized countries as to how to respond to countertrade even in a very general way. This reflects the genuine complexity of countertrade as a phenomenon—and the fact that barter-type trade is neither all good nor all bad. It is, however, something with which we are going to have to live and understand if we are going to be competitive and be able to maintain our trade flows with some semblance of order and progress.

U.S. GOVERNMENT SERVICES

The U.S. Department of Commerce has trade development and international economic policy officials who can be helpful on an operational basis in directing you toward other private-sector sources that might be able to help with countertrade or in providing basic information that would help you to reach a decision, unblock a problem, or direct you to another government agency that might be able to help. The State Department also has desk officers who can be very helpful. The U.S. International Trade Commission (USITC) was mentioned in chapter 2. In late 1984 the USITC sent a countertrade survey questionnaire to some 400 U.S. companies. A similar questionnaire was sent in 1985 on military offsets.

You may want to develop some contact with the United States Trade Representative's (USTR) Office. The USTR is politically sensitized to the countertrade issues. When you take a problem to USTR, it may have policy implications for them, but also it may be able to help you from the policy standpoint.

CONCLUSIONS

There are really no clear guidelines yet as to what course the U.S. government and others will take relative to barter. What we are seeing is a change in the methodology of trading or a fundamental change in the trading relationships of countries and companies. We are seeing reciprocity *assumed*, where before it was an added factor. We are seeing countries turning investments in one product almost automatically in some cases into investments of their choice in other products. We are seeing governments that, for example, engage in imports in government procurement, using that leverage to attain desired investments in industries in their countries. We are seeing U.S. companies having to turn their blocked currencies and royalties into investments in these countries.

What does that mean for the smaller traders? It means that to be competitive on this basis in this atmosphere they are having to look at that extra factor, such as countertrade, that they may be able to put into their bid. We are really talking about self-defense in a competitive market. It is not just being required of us per se, but it is more as if the market itself is requiring it. There will have to be a great deal more analysis and thought on the subject, but as of now, the chief concern of the U.S. government with respect to countertrade is its trade-distorting impact.

22

Countertrade: A View from the World Bank

NEIL R. ROGER

There is no World Bank view on countertrade in the sense that countertrade is not an issue that has been discussed formally at the board or even at the staff level. Countertrade is one of a number of trading issues that are discussed in various forums, but there is no particular accepted view.

BACKGROUND

I work as an economist in the World Bank in what is called "The Economics and Research Staff" (ERS). The ERS is responsible for ongoing research and analysis on matters of economics and development and provides advice to regional operating departments, particularly on economic policy matters, which is what I am largely concerned with. So I come to countertrade not as a practitioner but with a view to what countertrade means in economic-policy terms.

Focus upon Economic Development

The World Bank is a development-financing institution that has lent some $10 billion to $12 billion in recent years. The bank also has a strong role in advising developing countries on their economic policies. Indeed, recently there has been more emphasis on the bank's approach in encouraging countries to change their economic policies. A growing amount of the bank's personal and financial resources is directed toward what we call "program lending"—which is nonproject lending—supporting structural adjustment and policy reform in developing countries.

Thus my comments are made from the perspective of working in an organization that has a focus promoting economic development and a concern to encourage better economic policymaking. The World's Bank's general stance is protrade: trade is seen as a positive force for development, and the bank favors making trade as free as possible.

Trade issues were at the forefront of the discussions at a 1985 meeting of the Development Committee, a joint advisory committee of the World Bank and the International Monetary Fund (IMF). The emphasis of one of the background papers produced for the Development Committee meetings by the bank is the worrisome growth of nontariff barriers to trade in the world—in both developing and industrial countries. The thrust of the paper is that trade barriers reduce economic efficiency and inhibit growth and development and thus are generally undesirable. Nontariff barriers, which are complex and lack transparency, are particularly undesirable. The aim is to come up with methods to get rid of these barriers to trade.

Focus upon National Welfare and Efficiency

My focus is on developing countries, and when looking at countertrade, I am concerned with a national point of view and less concerned with the view of international trading companies and domestic firms. In a policy sense, I am concerned with what a developing country should be thinking about when it is considering introducing countertrade schemes. When I refer to "countertrade schemes," I am considering the whole range but mainly mandatory counterpurchase schemes like Indonesia's. Countertrade can be seen as a government-imposed trading rule, one of a whole range of policies that impact on trade.

When I refer to a "national view," I mean some notion of the overall well-being of the community. That is very much driven by how communities use their scarce productive resources. We should be concerned that scarce productive resources be used as efficiently as possible and therefore try to promote policies, particularly trade policies, that encourage efficiency.

This is not an ideological view. Economic theory indicates that national welfare will be served by encouraging resources to be allocated where they can be used most efficiently and by taking advantage of opportunities for trade. It is also a view that comes from the evidence. When we look at the performance of developing countries over time, the evidence supports the desirability of open trading relationships. Those countries that have maintained relatively liberal trade regimes have been more successful in terms of economic growth and handling shocks from the international trading system than have countries with more restrictive trading policies.

COUNTERTRADE

Economists are often concerned with policy alternatives. Countertrade is seen as just one of many alternative policies that could be used by developing countries to deal with their trading, payments, and other economic problems.

Reasons for Countertrade

Trading and payments difficulties: A common view of why the developing countries are interested in countertrade is the current trading and payments difficulties that many are experiencing. This is manifested in shortages of foreign-exchange reserves. How does countertrade affect the trading and payment difficulties? The common assertion is that it can somehow save foreign exchange or preserve foreign-exchange reserves for high-priority uses.

However, it is hard to support such claims. The goods going both ways are clearly tradeable—they are goods that enter international trade. In most instances the relative importance of the countertrading countries in world trade is small, and they cannot affect the price of the goods in world markets. Thus it is hard to see how countertrade by itself—simply the linking of the two transactions at given world prices—changes the foreign-exchange position of particular countries. Very clearly, it can change the foreign-exchange position of individual firms and traders, but it is far from clear that it changes the aggregate position of the country as a whole.

Export promotion: A second argument that is often cited about countertrade for developing countries is that it gives a modus operandi for export promotion. The export performance of many developing countries has been poor recently. But why has it been poor? The unsatisfactory performance is primarily due to policy reasons—their own policies and the policies of their trading partners.

Developing countries' trade policies consistently and very significantly tend to be biased *against* export activities. The two main things that are involved here are (1) overvalued and inconvertible currencies and (2) protection of import-substitution industries. These policies reduce the relative profitability of exporting and, therefore, are biased against exports.

How would countertrade serve to promote exports? The basic notion is that it works as a tax-subsidy scheme. Imports are taxed and exports are subsidized by means of the countertrade scheme, on an ad hoc transaction-by-transaction basis. However, if export promotion is the goal, countertrade is a very clumsy tool: it works for some products and for some firms. If we want to promote exports, there are much simpler and much preferred ways of doing it—specifically, devaluation and reduction of import protection, both of which increase the relative attractiveness of exporting. But such actions are very hard to do not only for developing countries but also for developed countries.

Exchange controls: A third suggested rationale for countertrade is that it can build some flexibility into the controls that are associated with overvalued exchange rates, particularly the rationing of foreign exchange and import quotas. Again, it is true that for particular firms and particular deals, it does build some flexibility into the controls. It may not be great, but it offers flexibility and a means for continuing business. But from the national point of view, it is hard to see that this is the most secure route to introducing flexibility. Very clearly, the way to introduce flexibility is to get rid of those controls and get back to a normal trading and payments regime for all participants.

Price controls: A fourth suggested reason for why developing countries are involved in countertrade is from the desire to disguise prices involved in some transactions. This is primarily relevant for commodities—for example, oil or sugar—that are subject to international marketing agreements or pricing formulas. Countertrade is seen as one means of chiseling on prices or otherwise getting around international agreements. What each country has to do is look at its long-term and short-term objectives with regard to these rules. Countertrade, although it is one way of getting around these things, may not always be the best way.

Development: A fifth idea is some sort of positive industry-development notion. By targeting particular types of industries or particular types of projects and building them into a countertrade framework, commentators suggest that countries can speed up development. Some countries have made some very clever decisions at opportune times and have brought out strong, striving industries. But in developing countries, there is also very strong evidence of poor choices of which industries to target and which industries to protect. Almost every developing country has a legacy of industries of little or no value.

Arguments against Countertrade

Even if we thought we were good at choosing the sorts of industries that a developing country should get into or in which it should expand, would countertrade be an efficient way of doing it? Generally, we would say no, because it is a complex and nontransparent means of protection to encourage a particular industry. Again, there are preferred routes to encouraging "infant" industries—for example, direct subsidies.

OVERVIEW

From the national point of view, there seems to be little gain in countertrade. Why then do we think of countertrade and why then reportedly do we see such an increase in it recently? From my point of view, it is fairly clear: there is a reluctance to face hard decisions in the reforming of exchange and trade regimes. This requires hard decisions and painful adjustment. Mandatory countertrade, among other trading policies, comprises a whole range of little fixes at the margin that may delay or otherwise put off less palatable and more comprehensive adjustments.

Mandatory countertrade distorts trade and the economy by raising costs and restricting choices. However, the degree of distortion from countertrade is probably relatively small. The sort of distortions that we should be more concerned about are the fundamental distortions that give rise to the incentives for countertrade—specifically, overvalued exchange rates, rationing of foreign exchange, and very complex and restrictive import controls.

Recommendations

What is the best approach to improving these things? The standard advice we should give to all developing countries is to get rid of controls and minimize the distortions in trading and payments policies. As Frederick Howell said in chapter 21, it is very important to try to get government out of qualitative controls on trade.

Again, I would stress that this is not an ideological view: it is a view of the experience of history. Some governments (people often use the example of South Korea) have been successful at manipulating some parts of their trade. But most of the evidence is that when governments become closely involved in trade and particularly when they impose discriminatory and complex restrictions on trade, the country as a whole tends to lose out. This is not to say that individual traders lose out; indeed, individuals can do very well with countertrade, but the nations as a whole—no. The standard advice to developing countries should be to free up their trade and payments regime and to take away the incentives of countertrade.

23

The Role of Countertrade in Future GATT Deliberations

MICHAEL R. CZINKOTA

Countertrade transactions, or at least talk about them, are occurring with increasing frequency. This fact has raised a particularly significant concern, namely, that countertrade represents a threat to the free, multilateral, global trade framework.

It is the purpose of this chapter to evaluate how countertrade transactions are currently compatible with the General Agreement on Tariffs and Trade (GATT) framework and what, if any, action should be undertaken by GATT to regulate countertrade.

THE NATURE OF GATT

GATT was designed to increase world trade, initially focusing on a reduction of tariff barriers and later on nontariff issues. The basic tenet of GATT was, and is, that to achieve the benefits of a world trade system, bilateral transactions based on noneconomic considerations must be replaced by a nondiscriminatory, multilateral approach with transactions completed on the basis of economic efficiency. At the same time, GATT recognized the special situation of the less developed countries (LDCs) and provided a variety of exemptions to help them increase their participation in world trade and to allow them means to develop and overcome currency shortages and balance-of-payments difficulties. The GATT, therefore, was conceived in the spirit of opening up world markets and allowing for gradual participation of all countries in the benefits of trade.

To assess the relevance of countertrade for the GATT, it is necessary to consider the issue of jurisdiction. The sole fact that some observers may not like countertrade or may feel that it is harmful to the intention of the GATT framework does not automatically mean that any practically sound and legally appropriate reason exists for the GATT to attempt to control and regulate countertrade transactions. Since the GATT represents an agreement between nations, specific violations of specific articles must exist for any GATT action to even be considered.

The GATT regulates the interaction of trade between governments. Keep in mind that this discussion is only relevant to barter transactions to which governments are parties. If private firms were to agree to countertrade arrangements among themselves as part of a commercial or noncommercial transaction, based on economic or noneconomic considerations, there would not be any policy implication for the GATT. Therefore, we must conclude that the jurisdiction for any possible GATT measure extends itself only to transactions in which governments participate, or mandated countertrade.

POSSIBLE GATT VIOLATIONS OF BARTER

Even when narrowed down to only the mandated transactions, there appear to be several GATT tenets that are violated. One issue of significance is that of transparency, which forms a basic dimension of the GATT. The GATT signatories believed that government interference in trade should be made overtly (or transparently), thus letting other trading partners know the extent of any trade-interfering practice. This way, it is hoped, future negotiations would be made easier and traders would have to deal only with the known rather than the unknown.

Countertrade requirements are often not transparent but are made quietly to the foreign company during the negotiating period; the commitment country's demands are often not open but secretive. As several of the earlier chapters have indicated, because there is no official specification or sorting of countertraded goods, no one knows exactly how much barter actually occurs. Many countries keep a very low profile, for example, by not issuing any countertrade regulations and not even sanctioning countertrade officially, yet making it clear that awards of import licenses and export performance are linked at the level of the firm. This raises questions such as how open was the bidding for a sale? Were all parties aware of the countertrade requirements? How was the issue of price and quantity settled? This reduction in transparency clearly inhibits the growth of world trade, particularly with regard to the equitable participation of the different trading partners.

A second major tenet of the GATT that seems to be violated by countertrade is the fact that such transactions encourage the spread of bilateralism. We must recall that the most fundamental principle of the GATT in the interests of economic growth was that of multilateral, nondiscriminatory trade. Countertrade limits transactions to the weakest party's ability to import. Since uncompetitive goods may be marketed, the opportunity for competition from other parties is reduced or eliminated. Trade then results from the ability of two countries to purchase specified goods from one another. As Paul Samuelson, the Nobel laureate in economics, has stated so appropriately: "Instead of there being a double coincidence of wants, there is likely to be a want of coincidence; so that, unless a hungry tailor happens to find an undraped farmer, who has both food and a desire for a pair of pants, neither can make a trade."[1] Instead of balances being settled on a multilateral basis, surpluses from one country balanced by deficits with another, accounts are settled on a country-by-country or even trans-action-by-transaction basis.

A third underlying dimension of the GATT to be considered is the reduction of trade distortions. As Neil Roger noted in chapter 22, since there are many hidden costs in countertrade transactions, such as administrative costs associated with having to market the countertraded products, costs hidden in the risk of delivery and in the quality of the product delivered, normal trade relations can be easily undercut. Because countertrade often takes place with goods that cannot be easily sold on the market, it restricts the ability of countries and their industries to adjust structurally to more efficient production. The overall result of such arrangements may be that inefficient producers are allowed to continue to flourish while more competitive producers disappear. Such trade distortions, in addition to violating the GATT, cannot even be justified based on the notion that they primarily help lesser developed countries. On the contrary, they may harm these countries in the long run by disrupting their normal trade relations and by not pushing them to adjust production into more efficient sectors of the economy.

Apart from these possible inconsistencies with the general tenets of the GATT, several specific articles may be violated by countertrade transactions. For example, the most-favored-nation principle and the principles of nondiscrimination stated in Article I of the GATT may be violated if a barter requirement is not applied uniformly to all trading partners. If the access to a country's market is conditioned on an exporter's purchase of an equivalent amount of the country's goods, the result is a bilateral system of trade, or exactly what the unconditional most-favored-nation principle tries to prevent.

In a similar fashion, the schedules of concessions, Article II, may be violated. Protection is not to exceed that provided for in the schedule. Unless the contracting party has included countertrade requirements as a condition in its schedule, a violation may be present.

The national treatment principle of Article III may also be violated through discrimination against imported products. An importer that can import only with a commensurate export is worse off than a domestic producer that does not have to satisfy such a requirement.

Article IX of the GATT prohibits any restrictions on imports or exports except for duties, taxes, or other charges. Quotas and licenses are prohibited. In the case of countertrade requirements, when a country limits imports to the subsequent exports, the requirement may constitute such a violating restriction.

If countertrade products are specified, a violation of the subsidies code of Article XVI may also occur. A countertrade requirement may artificially subsidize an export by linking it to an imported product. Although this applies only to nonprimary products, a prohibited subsidy to a primary product can also be construed as resulting from countertrade transactions. Countertrade may increase exports and take an unequitable share of the market, thus displacing other competitors, a practice that is in violation of the GATT. However, arguments could be made that the latter situation may not represent an actual violation particularly in cases of developing countries, since the GATT stipulates that the trade, development, and financial needs of developing countries need to be considered in applying its articles.

Finally, an argument for violation of Article XXVIII could be made, which stipulates that state trading enterprises must operate on a nondiscriminatory basis for government measures affecting imports or exports by private traders and that all purchases and sales must be made solely according to commercial considerations. A countertrade requirement not issued on all interested parties violates this article. Similarly, insofar as countertrade is not transacted according to solely commercial considerations, it may be a violation of this article.

POLICY CONSIDERATIONS

There appear to be various indications that the trade transactions mandated by government may be in violation of the GATT spirit and specific articles as noted above. This is confirmed by public statements of the GATT staff, which indicate that they are opposed to countertrade transactions, based on broad considerations of macroeconomic efficiencies. These authorities complain that instead of a rational system of exchange based on product, quality, and price, countertrade introduces extraneous elements into the sales equation and threatens the viability of the GATT.[2] For GATT to take action, however, there needs to be a constituency that presses the issue.

The Attitude of the U.S. Government

In looking at U.S. policy with regard to countertrade, it appears that the United States will not be the country to push the issue. There is a clear lack of coherence between the views of the Departments of the Treasury, Commerce, and Defense, the United States Trade Representative (USTR), the current and previous administrations, and U.S. business.

Most of these participants seem to recognize that countertrade is an inefficient, trade-distorting phenomenon, but as Frederick Howell noted in chapter 21, various elements of the U.S. government are very reluctant to take a strong stand against it—particularly Commerce, Defense, and the administration. Instead, they seem to prefer to find ways to make business more profitable under the circumstances of countertrade proliferation.

Strong statements against countertrade can be heard from the USTR, who found that "barter is a return to a bilateral system of trade at a time when the international community is seeking to safeguard a widened multilateral trading system."[3] They find this disadvantageous even for developing countries, since if these countries barter their exports instead of sell them, they reduce foreign exchange available to repay foreign debt. However, in an overall conclusion, the Trade Policy Review Group, headed by the USTR, recommends only that "the U.S. Government exercise caution in the use of its barter authority, reserving it only for those situations which offer advantages not offered by conventional market operations."[4]

The Department of the Treasury believes that countertrade may "have adverse effects on future U.S. production, trade, employment, and tax revenue."[5]

The Department of Commerce exhibits a much more ambiguous view of countertrade. Although some officials recognize the trade distorting effects of countertrade, they appear much more interested in aiding U.S. businesses in competitively dealing with such requirements. According to a Commerce Department countertrade expert, bilateral agreements are a "fact of life not only in East–West, North–South trade, but in trade among developed countries like France, Italy, and Japan that have entered into all sorts of un-GATT-like arrangements."[6] Former Assistant Secretary of Commerce for Trade Development Richard McElheny stated that countertrade was inefficient but he would not advise the government to interfere and possibly jeopardize U.S. business in its ability to participate competitively.

The Department of Defense in turn frequently imposes offset requirements under which it requests that foreign suppliers use their best efforts to hire U.S. subcontractors and purchase components from U.S. suppliers. It believes that U.S. industry is in the best position to decide whether or not to enter into such offset guarantees and to what extent and that firms may have lost a number of commercial transactions had they not agreed to significant offset requirements.

The Carter administration lambasted the effect of countertrade, calling these transactions "purely bilateral in nature, and uncompetitive since they squeeze out competition from third markets or specify the export market."[7] Subsequently, the Reagan administration appears to have taken a more pragmatic approach and currently seems to be unsure whether it should "try to hold the spread of countertrade or help the U.S. companies get their share."[8]

Given this current disarray within policy toward countertrade, it appears unlikely that the United States will be the GATT member to bring the matter to the forefront.

The Attitude of Other Industrialized Countries

A second group that could encourage the GATT Secretariat to work on the issue would be the other industrialized countries. However, this appears unlikely as well. In an unofficial statement by an European Community (EC) representative, countertrade appears to be viewed by the EC as a fact of life. The EC tends to take the view of the Organization of Economic Cooperation and Development (OECD) that countertrade is not an efficient mechanism for world trade but can be a second best solution when restrictions to traditional forms of trade arise. For this reason, the EC would not be in favor of changing the current rules of the GATT to regulate what the EC believes is a short-term phenomenon.

Action is also unlikely by other industrialized countries, since it is known that in addition to Western Europe, Japan and other countries such as Canada, New Zealand, and Australia have participated, some actively, in the growing countertrade phenomenon. According to the International Trade Commission (ITC) report released in 1982, the "catalysts for such (countertrade) arrangements are often the governments of Japan and those of Western Europe."[9]

The Attitude of Developing Countries

A final group that could initiate actions are the lesser developed countries. However, they are, due to financial constraints, clearly the ones most active in the countertrade field. Their inability to trade for hard currency is what gave rise to countertrade beyond the Eastern Bloc. It therefore seems unlikely that these countries would initiate any kind of GATT action. Also, some of the countries that are most deeply involved in countertrade, such as Mexico or the Soviet Union, are not part of the GATT. Therefore, they not only would be unwilling but also would be unable to raise the issue in the GATT forum.

It appears, therefore, that GATT action by its constituency is unlikely. In fact, the reason that the GATT has no official position on countertrade is mainly a result of the diversity of the views among the contracting parties.

PRACTICAL CONSIDERATIONS

Several practical considerations also make it appear unlikely that the GATT will undertake any action with regard to countertrade.

First, what case would be used and what evidence could possibly be brought forth? A trade deal that one enterprise may lose due to a countertrade requirement is difficult to prove on any case-by-case basis. In addition, challenging the trade transactions on the basis of transparency and discrimination could open the internal buying processes of multinational corporations to scrutiny. They may lack transparency in a similar fashion by not opening licenses to third parties. The danger of such a discussion would rapidly result in a large constituency in favor of abandoning these discussions.

Second, particularly as far as the United States is concerned, issues other than countertrade have much higher priorities for inclusion in any kind of GATT agenda or new trade round discussions—issues such as technology transfer, trade in services, and perhaps even agriculture. LDCs in turn are much more concerned about market access than they are concerned about countertrade. Overall, increasingly the interlinkage between exports and imports will be of concern in the GATT discussions. Therefore, it seems unlikely that too much energy will be expended in trying to bring countertrade issues to the table.

Attacking countertrade as an undesirable qualitative restriction would also not be looked upon very favorably by many industrialized countries. Such discussions could easily spill over into currently existing quantitative restrictions such as quotas and "voluntary" market agreements. These transactions, which at this time have taken place subtly outside of the GATT framework, would suddenly become part of the GATT discussions. Clearly, many industrialized countries, and not just the United States, would seem unwilling to let the discussions progress to this stage.

Another very practical consideration is the fact that by discussing countertrade, the practice would be dignified by official recognition. Since it would seem very unlikely that such discussions would result in a total abolishment of countertrade, regulations would be drafted by the GATT. These regulations by an international body would tend to institutionalize the practice of countertrade, a result that certainly seems undesirable for many countries.

Even if the issues were brought up at the GATT, it would be easy for many LDCs to claim exemptions from any kind of rulings because of balance-of-payment crises. Even when the issue is raised with regard to state trading and the requirement for commercial consideration, the LDCs involved could still insist that in fact they do base their transactions on commercial considerations only, since countertrade to them makes the difference between no trade and some trade.

Finally, it must be considered that even if countertrade were to be included under the GATT, the dispute mechanism of the GATT is far too unwieldy to handle most transactions. It often takes years to settle a dispute, and for most countertrade transactions, by the time the issue is considered, the transaction has long since transpired and the dispute is irrelevant.

THE REAL PROBLEM

As the aforementioned discussion shows, it would be unrealistic to expect the GATT to take on countertrade jurisdiction even though there may be some violation of the GATT spirit and specific GATT articles by these transactions. This is mainly based on the fact that both policy as well as practical considerations make such an action unlikely.

This result should not be particularly disconcerting for countertrade transactions in general, since in many instances, they are short term, are sufficiently small, and therefore do not affect the world trading system in a major way. However, there are several instances to consider in which supervision and a regulation by the GATT or another international regulatory agency (perhaps to be formed) would be appropriate. This is the case for both offset and compensation transactions. First, both of these types of transactions are long lasting.

Second, they also tend to be larger transactions that do affect world trade flows and the overall world economy. For example, offset amounts increasingly exceed the amount of the initial business transaction. Since military expenditures most often trigger offset requirements and seem to be on the increase for the foreseeable future, the problem appears to be longer lasting and one of increasing significance.

Compensation or buy-back agreements are increasingly demanded by countries seeking to attain development and transfer of technology. These types of transactions may distort world trade flows since many of the large projects developed under compensation agreements subsequently flood the market with products. An ITC report warns that the West may lose its export markets in the petrochemicals area due to overcapacity resulting from countertrade agreements.[10] This has already been seen in the steel industry, which currently suffers a worldwide recession. Such distortions may very well be threatening to the world trade framework.

Proliferation of barter presents very real problems for the spirit of the GATT in its attempt to increase world trade and improve the well-being of nations and individuals. This situation speaks very strongly for including countertrade under the GATT jurisdiction. However, there appears to be a difficulty of finding a single constituency or group of constituencies to step forward to attack countertrade.

CONCLUSIONS

In a general sense, it is appropriate to say that there is no reason for the GATT to take a strong stand against proliferation of countertrade or to attempt to bring it under its jurisdiction by issuing guidelines and regulations. The main reason for the conclusion is the fact that the incidence of countertrade has increased because of fundamental difficulties in the world economy. Proliferation of countertrade is a symptom of world economic difficulty rather than the problem in itself. Access to developed markets for the LDCs has become increasingly limited. Balance-of-payment crises, debt problems, and other financial difficulties have hurt the ability of the LDCs to import needed products. In the face of limited trade opportunities, LDCs as well as developed countries appear to regard countertrade as an alternative solution to no trade at all. Countertrade may be considered as a complementary or additional rather than alternative kind of multilateral trade. Given the structural economic difficulties of today, the immediate benefits of countertrade may make some of its negative aspects simply irrelevant.

In addition, it can be expected that growth of countertrade will at some point be halted by its own inefficiencies. Both buyers and sellers will compare their deals with the cash alternatives and will become disillusioned about their ability to separate and enlarge markets.

However, as far as offset and compensation agreements are concerned, there should be serious consideration for possible international regulation. The amounts involved are too large, and the trade-distorting effect too significant, to ignore the increase of these practices. Given the problematic situation already existing in the steel area, and probably emerging soon in other industrial sectors, it appears that should a new round of trade negotiations take place, a tightly defined discussion of such large-scale, long-term transactions should be included.

For all other forms of countertrade, however, regulation by the GATT seems inappropriate. Such action would only drive it further underground, making transactions even vaguer and requiring simply more separate documents, rather than eradicating it. Instead of the GATT regulation of these transactions, the solution would seem a mutual effort to work toward recreating the advantages of a market economy and making these advantages apparent. Countertrade proliferation may be unfortunate, but it cannot be dealt with by attacking the symptom instead of the problem. Until that can be accomplished, barter is likely to continue.

NOTES

1. Paul Samuelson, *Economics*, 11th ed. (New York: McGraw-Hill, 1980), p. 260.

2. "GATT Director Dunkel Criticizes Trend Toward Unilateral Trade Law Interpretations," *U.S. Export Weekly*, July 20, 1982, p. 557.

3. Carmen Suro-Bredie, director of South-East Asian Affairs, United States Trade Representative, Testimony before the House of Representatives, Subcommittee on Sea Power and Strategic and Critical Materials, Committee on Armed Services, 98th Cong., 1st sess., October 9, 1983.

4. Ibid.

5. John D. Lange, Jr., director, Office of Trade Finance, U.S. Department of the Treasury, Testimony before the House of Representatives, Economics Stabilization Committee, Committee on Banking, Finance, and Urban Affairs, 97th Cong., 1st sess., September 24, 1981.

6. "New Restrictions on World Trade," *Business Week*, July 19, 1982, p. 119.

7. *Report of the President on Competitiveness*, Washington, D.C., 1980, p. V–45.

8. "New Restrictions on World Trade," p. 119.

9. "Analysis of Recent Trends in U.S. Countertrade," Report by the International Trade Commission, Investigation #332–125, March 1982, p. 20.

10. Ibid., p. 17.

Suggested Readings

Business International. *Threats and Opportunities of Global Countertrade*, 1983.

Business Trend Analysis, Inc. *The World of Countertrade*, 1983.

Countertrade in the World Economy. New York: Group of Thirty, 1985.

Ehrenhaft, Peter D. *Countertrade and Trading Companies: Trade Trends in the 80's.* Clifton, N.J.: Law and Business Inc., 1984

Jones, Stephen F. *North/South Countertrade Barter and Reciprocal Trade With Developing Countries*. Economist Intelligence Unit, Special Report No. 174, August 1984.

Kaikati, Jack G. "Marketing Without Exchange of Money." *Harvard Business Review*, November-December 1982, pp. 72–74.

Keller, Robert I. "The Taxation of Barter Transactions." *Minnesota Law Review*, December 1982, pp. 441–511.

Korth, Christopher M. "The Promotion of Exports with Barter." In *Export Promotion*, Michael R. Czinkota, ed. New York: Praeger, 1983, pp. 37–50.

Korth, Christopher M. "Barter—An Old Practice Yields New Profits." *Business*, September-October 1981, pp. 2–8.

McVey, Thomas B. "Countertrade: Commercial Practices, Legal Issues and Policy Dilemmas." *Law & Policy in International Business*, no. 1, 1984.

Organization of Economic Cooperation and Development. *Countertrade: Developing Countries Practices*. 1985.

Organization of Economic Cooperation and Development. *East-West Trade: Recent Developments in Countertrade*. 1981.

Outters-Jaeger, Ingelies. *The Development Impact of Barter in Developing Countries*. Organization of Economic Cooperation & Development, 1979.

United States International Trade Commission. *Assessment of the Effect of Barter and*

Countertrade Transactions on U.S. Industries. USITC Publication 1766. October 1985.

Verzariu, Pompiliu. *Countertrade, Barter and offsets*. New York: McGraw-Hill, 1985.

Verzariu, Pompiliu. *Countertrade Practices in East Europe, The Soviet Union and China*. U.S. Dept. of Commerce, April 1980.

Weigand, Robert E. ''International Nonmonetary Transactions: A Primer for American Bankers.'' *Banking Law Journal*, March 1979.

Weishaar, Wayne and Wayne W. Parrish. *Men Without Money*. New York: G. P. Putnam's Sons, 1933.

Welt, Leo. *Trade without Money: Barter and Countertrade*. Clifton, N.J.: Law & Business Inc., 1984.

Index

About the Contributors

JAMES M. BARKAS is vice-president of Midland International Trade Services Corporation (MITS), a subsidiary of Midland Bank. Before joining MITS, Barkas worked at the First National Bank of Chicago and Chase Manhattan in a variety of trade finance capacities, including countertrade. He received the MALD degree from the Fletcher School of Law and Diplomacy and an undergraduate degree from Princeton University.

PAUL E. BOLIEK is executive vice-president and business development manager-Eastern Europe at General Foods Trading Company. Boliek joined General Foods in 1972 as director of licensing. The development of General Foods' businesses in Yugoslavia, Comecon, and Anglophone Africa and the countertrade requirements in these areas has been an important part of his activities. He holds chemical and mechanical engineering degrees from Georgia Tech and Pennsylvania State University.

DON BONKER is a congressman from the state of Washington. A Democrat, he is serving his sixth term in the House of Representatives and is chairman of the Subcommittee on International Economic Policy and Trade of the House Foreign Affairs Committee and chairman of the House Export Task Force. He sponsored and helped work through Congress the Export Trading Company Act of 1982, the Export Administration Act of 1985, and the Trade and International Economic Policy Act of 1986. Bonker is a graduate of Lewis and Clark College.

WILLIS A. BUSSARD is the executive director of the U.S. Association of

Countertrading Corporations. Bussard gained experience in worldwide sourcing and countertrade while working for Univex, IBM, United Brands, National Bulk Carriers, and the Société Générale de Serveillance. He serves on the Advisory Board of the World Trade Institute and has directed several surveys of the countertrade activities of major corporations. His chapter in this book is based upon the most recent survey.

BERNARD E. CONOR was president of International Trade Operations, AMF, until his retirement in September 1984. Conor currently acts as a consultant to international businesses. In his twenty-five years of management experience, he was responsible for establishing many of AMF's overseas subsidiaries. He is a member of the New York District Export Council of the U.S. Department of Commerce and chairman of the Exports and Jobs Committee. Conor also lectures at Pace University on International Business Affairs.

RICHARD V. L. COOPER is partner-in-charge of international trade services at Coopers & Lybrand. Cooper's responsibilities include advising clients on how to conduct international business, and he has advised foreign governments and American companies on how to cope with countertrade. Before joining Coopers & Lybrand in 1979, he was director of defense manpower studies for the Rand Corporation. Cooper has taught extensively and has served as a consultant to a wide variety of organizations. He is a member of the editorial board of ORBIS and the Board of Directors of the Washington International Trade Association. Cooper received the BA and MA degrees from the University of California-Los Angeles and the Ph.D. from the University of Chicago.

STEPHEN E. CRAIN is marketing director-North America for the Connaught Trading Company, a member of the Cadbury-Schweppes Group. Crain's responsibilities include marketing into North America the products sourced as a part of counterpurchases obligations by the Cadbury-Schweppes franchise managers out of certain central and Eastern European countries. He travels extensively with these Schweppes franchise managers to identify and negotiate for products that are marketable into North America. Crain spent four years with the countertrade group of Control Data and a year with a domestic barter house. He received the BA and MBA degrees from Brigham Young University.

MICHAEL R. CZINKOTA is the chairman of the National Center for Export-Import Studies at Georgetown University, where he also serves as a member of the faculty of marketing and international business. His area of specialization is trade policy. Czinkota's background includes eight years of business experience as a partner in an export-import firm and in an advertising agency and nine years of research and teaching in the academic world. He holds MBA and Ph.D. degrees from Ohio State University.

A. PATRICK GILES is the resident partner in London for the U.S. law firm of Lane and Mittendorf with its London corsortium Boodle and King. He holds AB and MBA degrees from Dartmouth and a JD degree from the University of Michigan. Giles was unable to present a paper at the International Countertrade Conference, but his chapter is included in this collection because of the interesting nature of the subject.

FRED T. GOLDBERG, JR. is a partner with the law firm of Skadden Arps Slate Meagher & Flom. Previously, he was chief counsel for the Internal Revenue Service (IRS) and had served as assistant to the commissioner and as acting director of the Legislation and Regulation Division. He joined the IRS from the accounting firm of Latham, Watkins and Hill. Goldberg's primary area of expertise is in international taxation. He holds JD and BA degrees from Yale University.

L. DUKE GOLDEN is president of PacCom Trading Corporation. Previously, he was vice-president of international business operations at the Northrop Corporation in charge of Northrop's worldwide offset program. Golden has been in international business for more than twenty-five years, first as chief counsel for Glidden International and then in different roles with the Kaiser Organization. He is a member of the President's Export Council of Northern California and holds memberships in other trade groups. Golden received the JD degree from Indiana University.

ROBERT HENREY is director of international tax consulting and a partner with the accounting firm of Coopers & Lybrand. He has responsibility for the development of the firm's nationwide international tax practice, which covers a broad range of corporate consulting. Henrey has had extensive experience in the commercial banking industry including project finance, Eurodollar bank syndications, and corporate finance. He received an academic degree from Oxford University.

FREDERICK E. HOWELL is an international economist in the Office of Multilateral Affairs, U.S. Department of Commerce (DOC). He has been with the DOC for ten years and has served as a delegate to the Organization for Economic Cooperation and Development (OECD). Before joining the DOC, Howell was an international management consultant.

MARY JANE IAIA-McPHEE is a member of the Financial Industries Group of Arthur D. Little, Inc. Before joining Arthur D. Little, she was manager-trade finance services at the Royal Bank of Canada, where she was instrumental in the development and management of the bank's Countertrade/Commodities Finance Group. At Arthur D. Little, she has been responsible for developing and managing an international trade and contertrade counsulting practice. She holds law and bachelors degrees from McGill University.

CHRISTOPHER M. KORTH is professor of international finance and banking at the University of South Carolina. He has taught at Pennsylvania State University and was director of research at the Institute of International Commerce of the University of Michigan. Between 1973 and 1977, he was assistant vice-president and chief international economist with the First National Bank of Chicago. Korth received a doctorate from Indiana University.

JEROME K. LEVY is director-reciprocal trade, The Mediators, Inc. His responsibilities include all trade that The Mediators makes with major foreign and domestic corporations. Levy has had more than ten years experience in the barter business.

CHRISTOPHER D. McFARLANE is managing director of the New York Bay Co., Ltd. Previously, he was a vice-president in Manufacturers Hanover Trust Company with responsibility for the bank's countertrade unit in the World Trade Center Group and had held positions in the Far East and London. He is a member of the National Foreign Trade Council and holds BA and MBA degrees from Colgate University and Sophia University, respectively.

THOMAS B. McVEY is an attorney with the law firm of Lane & Mittendorf, Washington, D.C. He is a specialist in international trade and investment. A member of the bars of the state of New York and the District of Columbia, McVey holds a bachelor's from Columbia University and a law degree from Georgetown University.

SETH MAEROWITZ is a member of the mergers and acquisitions group of Shearson Lehman. He was formerly a management consultant with the Financial Industries Group of Arthur D. Little, Inc., specializing in Latin America, international trade, and countertrade. Previously Maerowitz was with corporate lending at the Bank of America. He holds an MBA in international finance from the Sloan School, Massachusetts Institute of Technology.

KATE MORTIMER is a director of N. M. Rothschild & Sons Ltd, London, currently on assignment to the Securities and Investments Board (the proposed new regulatory agency for investment business in the UK) as policy director. At Rothchilds from 1984–85 her responsibilities included providing advisory services on project finance, especially natural resource projects, and general international corporate finance and consultancy service to governments and state entities. Before then, at Rothchilds, she was running a corporate treasury advisory service focusing on exposure management and similar services for central banks. She served on the Central Policy Review Staff of the UK government (1972–

78) and spent three years (1969–72) with the World Bank as a loan officer and economist.

FRANK A. OCWIEJA is vice-president, MG Services. Ocwieja was previously senior project manager with Chase World Information Services and Country Marketing Manager, Middle East and Africa, with the U.S. Department of Commerce. He holds a BSFS degree from Georgetown University and a MALD degree from the Fletcher School, Tufts University.

NEIL R. ROGER is an economist with the Economics and Research Staff of the International Bank for Reconstruction and Development, a position he has held for three years. His area of expertise is macroeconomic and trade policy. Roger joined the World Bank from a position with the Australian government dealing with trade and industry policy. His chapter is based on the paper "Countertrade: A Developing-Country Policy Perspective," The World Bank, 1985 (mimeo).

JACQUES ROSTAIN is vice-president and manager of trading with Combustion Engineering Trading, Inc. His responsibilities include developing third-party business in the fields of barter and countertrade. Rostain also develops outlets for new Combustion Engineering business. He was previously vice-president and manager of the Countertrade Department, European American Bank, and has held positions with Merban International and Continental Grain. He holds a BA degree from Yale University.

BARRY F. WESTFALL was formerly vice-president, Contitrade Services Corporation, a wholly owned subsidiary of Continental Grain Company. Westfall was responsible for coordination and management of worldwide countertrade activities. His activities included nontraditional trade finance, countertrade, barter, and clearing and switch transactions executed worldwide on behalf of multinational corporations and in coordination with Contitrade's regional offices. Westfall was previously owner and chief operating officer of a textile manufacturing and international trading company and a management consultant with Arthur Young. He holds BS and MBA degrees from the University of North Carolina-Chapel Hill.